THE BRIDPORT PRIZE

POETRY AND SHORT STORIES

JUDGES

Lynne Reid Banks • Short stories
George Szirtes • Poetry

First published in 2000 by
SANSOM & COMPANY
81g, Pembroke Road, Bristol BS8 3EA
Tel: 0117 9737207

ISBN 1 900178 38 9

British Cataloguing-in-Publication Data.
A catalogue record for this book is available from the British Library.

Typeset by Mayhew Typesetting, Rhayader, Powys and printed by Hobbs the Printers, Totton, Hampshire.

Contents

Contents

LYNN REID BANKS

Story Report

What exactly is a short story?

Well, I'll tell you what – in my opinion, which I give without apology – it is not.

It's not a memoire. It's not an excerpt from a longer work. It's not a synopsis for a television play, or a film. It's not a blown-up joke or anecdote. Nor is it a vignette. It's definitely not a rambling semi-abstract introverted piece of personal reflection.

What it is, is a tale. Old-fashioned word, suggesting boozy nights round a campfire, or Hans Christian Andersen. What else can I call it? An account, a history, a narrative, my thesaurus gives me all these, but none of them is quite right. Really, the word 'story' stands alone.

But to be a story, it has to have a plot, and to be a short story, it has to move along. It has to keep your nose to the page, your fingers ready to turn it swiftly, and your eyes away from the page-number. If you find yourself looking to see how many pages you've read or how many are left to go, there's something wrong. It has to tell you something new and make you believe it and it has to leave you perhaps surprised, or shocked, or moved, or amused, but withal *satisfied.*

So that implies good writing and a good plot and a good ending. This is hard graft even if you have talent. And although, as I've often said, anyone who is not illiterate, can write, and get pleasure from expressing themselves, that's not the same as being a good writer. Talent is rare and it jumps from the page. But even talented writers can write bad short stories. *And do.*

When I started to read the 63 stories that filtered through to me from the preliminary judging – which winnowed this number out of 2,751 entries – I was surprised and delighted to find that 60 of those 63 stories were worth reading. (I think the three were left in the pile by the preliminary judge as a small sample of what he had had to wade through.)

I enjoyed my task. It's a long time since I had the opportunity to read what amounted to a thick volume of short stories. (The last time, incidentally, was when I was asked to review a published book of Hebrew short stories in translation. My review began: 'I quit. I've read to page 307 and that's it. Reading is for pleasure.' I mention this to show that I am not all that easy to please.)

And as I read these 60 stories, which were of all kinds, from many backgrounds, and noted the high standard of sheer writing ability, some of it certainly of publishable level, I wondered that a number of very good authors had decided to enter a competition like this, to throw their work into a sort of melting pot in the hope of a relatively modest reward. I decided it must be because of the lamentable shortage of outlets for short-story writers these days. Gone are magazines such as *Argosy* and *Blackwood's* and *Cornhill* whose brief was to publish the cream of modern short-story writers, new and old. Alas, even mass-market magazines that once carried short stories and serials no longer do so. As for anthologies in volume form, 'There is not the market' say bottom-line conscious editors. Erstwhile readers get their 'stories' (with less effort) from TV. But this is a shame. And it is hard for writers to confine themselves to the markets that pay them an often scant living, when they may have a real bent for this particular medium – the short tale well told.

The importance of titles should not be underestimated. Titles draw a reader; I felt a frisson of interest when I picked up a story with an intriguing name. 'The Burning of the Blue-Winged Boys.' 'Midnight in Seville', 'Does She Like Word-Games?' '75 Practical and Pleasing Ways to Tie a Tie.' 'Double Sun', 'Lucy's Grasp of Japanese', and, one of the winners, 'Billy Brown of London Town and the Troglodytes of Bow.' Seldom was the promise of these titles not to some extent fulfilled; it seems people who dream up exciting titles have the imagination to make them good in the story they introduce.

But, to the stories themselves. Basically they were a satisfyingly diverse collection. There were stories set in Africa, America, Italy; in the present and in the distant past, one a saga of medieval times, plus of course the inevitable Sci-fi futurist ones. But there were themes which cropped up over and over again, so that I found myself, in my notes, beginning: '*Yet another* childhood memoire,' or 'another story narrated by a murderer.' The murder stories, on the whole, were less interesting than the childhood ones, though the latter were often diffuse and unstructured. It hurt a lot when I had to set a story atop the 'not prize material' pile because, despite a high mark for writing quality, the story did not fulfil my criterion of what a story ought to be – in other words, it didn't tell a tale.

I started by giving two distinct marks, one for writing and one for story. I found myself giving 8's and 9's and even 10's and I wondered how I was going to arrive at a judgement with so much good material, and then I came across one that was different from any I'd read so far. I didn't want to down-mark any of the earlier good ones, but this one demanded a third category and I couldn't exactly pin down what it was. It told a good story very well but it did more. It enlightened and uplifted me. It was, as my husband says tersely, *about* something. Something more than just – well, what it was about. *Stone Soup* is *about* an African woman whose horizons are broadened when her husband insists that his by-blow daughter join her household. But it's also *about* how women relate to each other across generations and education-lines and culture-lines. It's about how women learn to stand up to men, to reach out into a wider dimension, to lift themselves above the parapet of their own narrow lives. The concept of the 'stone soup' of the title is also beautiful and moving and enlightening. The quality this story had is that of an additional depth and width – it drew on a wider humanity.

The reason this story didn't win first prize was because every now and then this simple narrator who has no education 'forgot herself' and came out of character, letting the educated author's voice ring through, using words and phrases that 'Mama Julius' wouldn't know. But it was a very near thing.

Sometimes when I re-read the could-be-a-winner stories in the last stages of judging, I noticed errors in writing and grammar, or plotting, that I hadn't noticed at first, and had to mark them down. Questions arose in my mind that the author fudged. The first prize-winner, I figured, should be as nearly flawless as possible. And I do think *Giddy, Stick and the Beach Hut* is nearly flawless. Apart from the fact that I longed for Giddy and Stick to be friends at the end and go into the beach-hut and drink chocolate together and get warm, and almost wept when Stick slammed the door on Giddy, the artist in me – the human being – knew that, alas, it was the right ending and that my disappointment was due to the author having made me care so much about these two kids and hate their beastly little teenage persecutors, so sadly representative of the callous cruelty of young people, and want Stick not to become like them. It's a marvellous story, beautifully and concisely written.

The third prize was very hard to decide on. Sometimes when you've read a lot of stories that are examples of beautiful, lyrical writing, whose authors have a real gift with words, when you come to a story that is simply and straightforwardly told without any frills, you think, Hey, but where's the fancy stuff? And you remember that fancy stuff isn't necessary. The great short-story writers of the past, de Maupassant, Maugham, Saki, ee cummings, didn't bother with fancy stuff. They just told their tales, and we read them, riveted, and never forgot them. So much that's being written now – books, plays, stories – are so focussed on elaborate, clever writing-style (oh, and 'relationships') that they forget what a good story's all about. For my part, that's a pity.

So here I had about five good stories, all plain tales well told. One was about a young couple in a California bus-station who meet an old woman who lays a shadow on the young man's life by prophesying that his wife will die young. One was about a child whose sister has died and who tries to break through his parents' fixated grief to make them notice what they have left. (There was a clever twist in this one because you were sure the narrator was a girl, and there was a little authorial cheating here!) One dealt with two children and an old woman in Jersey who had had a baby by a German soldier and become a crazy outcast. It showed how the casualties of war go on and on like endless ripples.

Comedy is as hard in a short story as in any other form of writing. I laughed aloud at the story about a father of the future who makes the mistake of taking his four-year-old daughter on a trip to the moon, where she happily destroys the one true lunar tourist attraction – man's first footprint in the moon dust. I also enjoyed a nice comic story of an art-class in which the foibles of all the 'students' are revealed, and this had a touching surprise ending too.

But none of these had the humane and soul-expanding quality that I had begun to look for since reading *Stone Soup* and *Beach Hut*. *Los Gatos Bus* came closest and nearly got third prize but then I compared it with *Billy Brown of London Town and the Troglodytes of Bow*.

This *is* a memoire, but it's also a story, a wonderful story of a little boy who loses his entire family – not all at once but one after another – in the bombing of London in World War Two. It's not flawless. His feelings as these terrible disasters hit him are not satisfactorily described. I felt the author couldn't bear to get too close, but the evocation of war-time in the East End, the characterisations of his mother and father, the descriptions of events, the ending where he runs into the tunnel in the tube to escape the real world and join the mythical Troglodytes who may accept him or devour him, are masterly, and in the end outweighed in their scope and strength the other very good stories that are runners-up.

Of course if Bridport Arts had picked a younger judge, or a male judge, almost certainly other choices for the winners would have been made. But as St. Joan said, 'what other judgement can I judge by but my own?' I congratulate all the winners and many of the losers, thank them for giving me reading pleasure, and hope that one day I shall see a number of these stories where they belong – in print for many people to read.

GEORGE SZIRTES

Poetry Report

Usually it is when it gets down to the last fifty that it gets really hard. In this case it was down to the last two hundred. The discarding of the next hundred poems was tough but the job thenceforth became ever more difficult. I know this sounds sanctimonious ('You are such wonderful people, I love you all!') but when I had read and reread the last hundred or so several times it got so it hurt to discard any poem, not so much because every one was of an extraordinary, transcendent quality, but because each of them was not only very well written but had registered as a potent record of genuine human experience.

Poems are, I believe, the most intense way of reconciling our experience of the world to what we can say about it, and our experience of the world is endless: massive, minute, particular, poignant, breathtaking, surprising, humiliating, consoling, comic and tragic. Language, on the other hand, is slippery, ever deteriorating, ever changing, ever expanding, often blunt, usually misleading, but at the same time seductive, multi-coloured and multi-faceted. 'God knows where words go. / Dust to dust. / The poet likes and distrusts them. / Someone must.' I wrote somewhere and would only substitute 'loves' for 'likes'. Language is a wonderful disenchantment and poetry's task is to re-enchant it, so that we may believe not only in what words mean but the way they mean. (There was a fine book by the American poet John Ciardi published in the early sixties, with the title 'How a Poem Means' and that gets it about right.) The arbitrary sounds we build into the rhythmical, musical and associative patterns we call poems reconnect us to the world, so that when we hear a politician, a pundit, or a sloppy journalist droning on, we become ever more aware of how the words they are using peel away from the world they appear to describe.

So much greater then the pleasure of finding words that seem to carry the world convincingly with them. And it is, of course, a complex pleasure. We do not enjoy poems because we think the writer is a decent human being, because the poem talks about things we like or because it supports opinions that we approve of. We don't even enjoy them because the experience the writer talks about seems deep and worthwhile. We all have those experiences, not only the poets. Some of the deepest, most intense feelings, are contained in some of the most ill-written verse. We cannot know the nuances of another creature's feelings, and the failure to present them in language is only that and no more. A man who talks crudely may have the most complex feelings: in fact his crudeness may actually be the result of an inability to shape those feelings in language. We know this instinctively when we watch the eyes, listen to the tone of the voice and note the hesitations, the vacancies.

So, in judging this competition, I have not been overly concerned with subject matter or with the experience the poem refers to. A very fine poem about a twinge of lust is as valuable as a half-successful poem about justice, love, nature, history or visionary experience. I am not interested in thematic hierarchies, but in the minute, exhilarating truths of language. So would most poets be, I think, disillusioned old gumshoes that they are, and well used to walking the mean streets of language. No fine frills or good manners (nor indeed deliberately bad ones) will haze them. You can talk the talk but can you walk the walk, is the question.

Once you get to the last two hundred poems – those good, honourable, sometimes very moving poems that are technically more than competent, that can certainly walk the walk – you are beginning to look for something extraordinary, and the extraordinary is, by definition, rare. And here all kinds of accidental and subjective factors enter the equation. You have to read, re-read and take breaks, otherwise everything blurs. I am asked by the organisers to nominate very few poems indeed, and I worry that the poets who are not among that few may think their poems were easily discarded. It is not the case, and if it were a feasible exercise I would certainly append the names of at least fifty poems – I only have numbers for the authors, not names – as the tip of a reasonable iceberg, because this was certainly a good lot of submissions, and there were individual poets with several poems I found enjoyable. I discarded poems I liked a lot only because I had to – usually for some minor reason such as unevenness, a weak passage often in the middle of the poem, or a lapse of register at a particularly crucial point. Or because others excited me more at the time.

Before going on to the final short list I would like to record here the names, if no more, of some of the poems that vied for prizes: 'Yodelling', 'Aeroplanes', 'Old Money', 'Eclipse at Skara Brae', 'The Heart's December', 'After School', and, closely following them, 'Pushing the Envelope', 'Signs', 'Revelation', 'Sex Education', 'Up the Junction at Fahrenheit 451', 'My Mother's Cigarettes', 'Morning on Bridge Street' and 'The Silver Fish'. This wholly diverse set of poems moved and exhilarated me with high-spirits, intelligence, poignancy and sharpness of perception.

Competitions are quite specific platforms for poetry. The high prize money and the delicate differentials that result in large financial differences are just part of the package. However uneasy I sometimes feel about such things I have to admit that competitions are effective, useful for both public relations and talent spotting. How is that? If I read an individual book I am aware of entering a furnished world. The imagination can impose itself on the reader quietly, insistently, with mounting power. But books usually come about after some degree of prolonged success. A magazine or anthology cannot offer the sense of mounting power, but, since the range of voices available is necessarily narrower, it is possible to find admirable work at some leisure. A big prestigious competition like the Bridport is rather like working your way through a vast crowd. What one wants is fresh air, an imagination that strikes one first of all with its novelty or poise, then, on closer inspection, with its substance. Poems that take risks while remaining on their feet are at an advantage. The poems I have chosen for the final list all succeeded in surprising me, a great competition virtue, and left me curious about a potential body of work by the poets involved.

With this in mind, I want to register, briefly, my response to the six very fine poems that were prize winners or very close contenders:

'Visitors' does nothing particularly surprising with its diction, but it is acutely sensitive to the tremors of hope and fear in an ordinary domestic setting. The poem's notion of the adequate is as delicate as the birds that return like soft rain on stones, the 'frost-creak stir' of silence, the spider's footfall and the egg ticking. This adequateness is not easily bought: it is paid for with sacrifices of all sorts. The egg that ticks arrives like the lightest emblem of mortality that underlies what is adequate.

The dramas of 'Public Records Office' are the routine events of history. The subject tempts grandiloquence which is met here with steadiness of vision and the desire to discover some 'adequate' encompassing image. Here the runaway hackneys, train wrecks, the warships that 'broke like a biscuit' can transcend their status as items on a list of generalities. The shift to the final image is subtle and natural, but the sense of it is enormous: it is the enormity that is adequate here, in the uniting of images of fire and water and soot.

I have certain suspicion of the overt use of local idiom because, as an immigrant, I feel excluded by it and think it can be a cheap way of claiming direct street-voice authority. In *Ulysses* Joyce says something to the effect that God is a cry in the street. I agree with him but am not always persuaded that conscious written use of dialect is any more than it was for Eliot in *The Waste Land* or for Kipling in his *Barrack Room Ballads*. 'Cause', however, is spoken-voice writing at its best, and that usually means it is saying something so simple it demands to be rediscovered. It is a delicious poem that sweeps me off my feet. It's youthful without being modish. Its terms of reference are entirely conventional, and yet it comes up fresh, convincing, passionate and springlike. Good for Mackie, I say.

As to my prize-winners, 'Hush' is a poem about a flash (in this case, literally a flash) of understanding, an insight into death and the momentary brilliance of sheer existence. It begins in a known but potent lyrical rhythmical mode I am a sucker for, with rain and all its associations of cleansing and tears. The children burst on to a kind of theatre as the thunder approaches, then, with a penetrating sense of personal involvement, comes lightning. I know this feeling, recognise it, and am surprised by how intense the sense of recognition is.

The besetting fault of competence is lack of ambition. Ambition is easily accused: pretentiousness, incompetence, incoherence, arrogance, indecency are all charges that a Middle-England jury, accustomed to Larkin and elegy, are liable to bring against the Flash Harry or madman who dares to raise his swollen head above the parapet. 'Homage' is one of those mad poems. In terms of orthography it is careless, inconsistent, even messy, if only because it is spiritually windblown. And what is worse it claims to 'think for England'. Its thinking is of the visionary, passionate kind. Its nearest cousins are Christopher Smart, William Blake and Walt Whitman, and that makes it highly unusual. But it does think, intelligently, courageously and with a kind of rushing depth. I would have wished it a little less rushed in commonplace matters like punctuation, but I don't feel inclined to judge it by those standards.

Curiously enough, my winner begins almost exactly like 'Homage' with an 'I think', which is a risk-taking rhetorical act of self-consciousness. You'd better think something interesting after that. The writer of 'Snail Love with Opera' had produced another extraordinary poem on my short list that just lost me a little in the middle where it seemed to clog and slow, but even so, it showed a mind and sensibility that seemed to me wholly original: grotesque, sad, vivid, sensual, sensitive yet vibrant in a measure that took my breath away. My winning poem does what the writer's other poem did, but the energy goes all the way through. The vision is disturbing and original: freedom, imprisonment, Beethoven, Mozart, sliminess, sex, death, nature as a form of opera. It is uncomfortable and barely human, but compulsive as only certain sorts of truth can be. The energies of 'Homage' are as positive as the charge of Liberty on Delacroix's barricades, or, if that seems paradoxical for England, as the route of Chesterton's rolling English drunkard who made the rolling English road. The energies of 'Snail Love . . .' are darker, more involuted, more spectral, more Fuseli. I would not want darkness as a mannerism but I don't feel the poem's energies are at all mannered. They are new and shaking and vigorous. I am curious as to where such energies have been and where they will go.

VICTORIA WORSLEY

Giddy, Stick and the Beach-Hut

'But my clothes are in there!'

Silence.

'You can't do this!'

No response.

'Oh come on.'

Stiffled giggles. Silence.

Gideon risked a brief and desperate attack on the door. Too desperate.

Silence.

More giggles.

Obviously revealing desperation was a bad course. He should have know that. But he wasn't used to being treated like this. No one treated him like this at home. And it was bldy cold for god's sake. (He still couldn't quite say 'bloody' without half swallowing it, even in his thoughts)

Gideon slumped on the stone step and shivered violently in his swimming trunks. A slate sea threw up pebbles on a wintry beach. The brief spell of glorious April sunshine was subsiding into cloud cover sped on by a bitter North Sea wind. It would rain again soon. He began to loathe this stupid place.

The gas cannister fired up in the hut. They weren't allowed to do that either. Aunt Sal (Lou's Mum) had specifically said not to without an adult. Not that they cared. They'd be warming up in there. Warming up and steaming up the windows; slithering out of sticky, salty costumes; rubbing down pale, goose-pimply flesh; brewing up forbidden cocoa. And giggling at him. Whispering and giggling. Gideon clutched his bony knees and shook. He was beginning to loathe these stupid girls.

Two minutes. Five. Ten. Hours of cold though. His teeth clattered along with the teaspoons inside the hut. Perhaps he should just crawl back into the sea and swim to keep warm . . . . Perhaps not . . . . Surely they'd be out soon. They'd come out anoraks flapping, fishing for cigarettes (which they weren't meant to have either!). All elbows, boots, and gluey pony tails – and laughing at him. That's all they'd ever done since he arrived in this stupid, boring town. Laugh at him. What was so funny? He wasn't funny at home. At home he had a new keyboard. That wasn't so funny. A Yamaha JX20. His Dad got it in the sales. Ha bldy ha. Bet they didn't have one. Bet they didn't. And he had a Playstation – he'd already got to the teenage level in Zelda – and he'd done the Spirit Temple. Bet they hadn't. Girls are rubbish at video games. Bet they didn't even have a Playstation. He'd tell them when they came out. Not obviously. Just let it drop somehow. Let them know a thing or two. When they came out. They'd come out soon. Surely. Surely *something*. But nothing. Another five. Another ten. Might as well be days.

Suddenly a change – indignation broke out in the hut behind him: Jeers, calls – was that a shutter bolt maybe? He waited, ready, hopeful . . . But no. It subsided disappointingly into laughter again. He turned back to the bitter sea and even more bitter wind, jamming himself into the front of the hut to escape the cold – and felt an unexpected jet of warm, steamy air on his back. He turned again sharply to see the lower half of the hut door open – just a crack. He had a glimpse of skinny knees wrapped close before a great shout erupted, a towel jerked out and the door snapped tight again. More muffled shouts. The hut frothed with fury. Gideon clutched his prize round him, eager for more. The hut heaved with furious girlish revenge as Gideon waited – tense and hoping for his trousers. Finally the moment: The hut door opened fully to send out clouds of cocoa, puffs of heated-up sea, wafts of wet skin smell – and a small girl in a big towel. And then the hut snapped shut again, toasting its victors.

Laughter again. Still no trousers but at least a towel. Two of them now on the steps.

Stick huddled against the hut as far away from Giddy as possible. Sea spray – or was it the first drops of rain? – flung itself sporadically in her face. Hideous wind. She drew her towel up to her nose, and stared hard at her cold, sandy feet peeking out of the bottom. How to live this down? Dreadful boy. Wretched, bloody boy. This was his fault. Why did he ever have to turn up here? She didn't even like boys. Especially not the pathetic morons her own age. And doubly especially not this one with his 'I've got blah at home, what have you got?' crap. Now she was stuck with this wimpy git out here in the cold. Shit. She'd only suggested they let him into the outside but because of the cold wind and it had been 'No way, no boys allowed' and 'What, you on his side now? Disloyal traitor'. That should have told her. (She might not have been too sure about the details of the 'Diswhatever' bit, but the general intention was clear.) But even if they weren't going to let him into the outside they shouldn't have minded him having a towel, should they? Shit. It had been going pretty well till then. Them being dumped with Lou's dickhead cousin for a few days had at least made her more like one of them. Shit, shit, shit. He even had a pathetic, wet, crapoid name. What on earth had made her help him?

Stick kept herself turned fiercely away from Giddy. Her tangly hair hung in obstinate strings of seaweed down her bony back. Minutes passed. Nothing. Stick's bony back shivered a little.

'Thanks for the towel,' Giddy tried. Stick's back didn't budge.

'Wasn't me . . . What towel?'

'Of course it was you.'

'Wasn't.'

'Was.' Stick glanced over her shoulder just enough for him to see her red beacon of a nose and rapidly blueing lips, set off by her thin white face.

'Why would I give you a towel?'

'Why else would they throw you out?'

'They didn't.'

'Looked like it to me.'

'So? I wanted to come outside.'

'Rubbish. You're not even dressed yet.'

Stick stuck her scary face in his and hissed: 'At least I've got my knickers!'

Giddy didn't feel able to answer that one. He wasn't sure if he was relieved she'd got her knickers or alarmed by the implication that she hadn't got anything else. He wasn't sure it was something he wanted to think about. Stick was younger than the other girls (about his age) and smaller. But it didn't make her any nicer to deal with, he decided, even if she had thrown him the towel. Especially not with a face like that – nor a body, come to that. (They didn't call her 'Stick' for nothing. Although he'd noticed when they were swimming how her pot-belly protruded in a very un-stick-like fashion and how, below her as yet non-existent tits, her rib cage stuck out like slipped breasts.)

Still she was his only potential ally against the older girls locked up with his clothes in the steamy hut. He'd learnt not to count on his cousin for anything, but one of the others (Mags or Maz or some weird name) was Stick's big sister. Surely she wouldn't let her stay out here for any length of time. With or without her knickers.

But the hut stayed shut. Its shutters stayed shut. Its door stayed shut. It was a decidedly shut up hut. The only thing to come out of it was a slight oozing of salty, chocolatey warmth.

Stick didn't move. They'd be getting dressed now. In there. Fixing bra straps, jamming on tee shirts, yanking on jeans. Babs would be inexplicably powdering herself everywhere first.

'Next year,' thought Stick, 'next year it'll be alright. Next year I'll be thirteen. Next year I'll be a teenager like them and everything will be alright. I'll have caught up. I'll be the same as them. I'll be one of the gang. No questions.'

'I thought you were a boy when I first saw you yesterday.' Giddy tried a new approach.

'So?'

'So nothing – you just . . . look like a boy.'

He'd thought she might be flattered but he'd clearly been wrong.

'You look like a girl.' She spat it at him nastily.

'Don't.'

'Do.'

'Don't.'

'Why've you got long hair then?'

'It's not long. It's just curly. When it's wet it sort of uncurls that's all.'

'Curly like a girly. And I don't look like a boy. Boys are crap. You're crap.'

'You're bldy rude.'

'And you're fucking wet.'

Shocked into silence, Giddy turned abruptly away. Two faces burnt with cold and anger. Two fiercely bony backs together. The wind yanking cruelly at the precious towel they hugged to their skinny frames. The hut – a placid palace of smug calm behind. And so it was for a while: cold hatred and freezing anger reigned outside while the hut kept its toasty teenage secrets wrapped up close inside.

Until Stick felt something tweak her toe. It was shame. Or shame's little sister, or something altogether a bit smaller than shame, but that nevertheless managed to tweak her toe just a little. The same small relation of shame that had made her hand throw Giddy a towel not long ago. After all it wasn't really his fault he had been dumped on them for these few days. It wasn't really his fault he was a pale, scrawny thing with yukky little tight fluorescent swimming trunks that looked like pants and showed his bits (eergh!), it wasn't his fault he'd been shut out, it wasn't even his fault he showed off about his pathetic Playstation. Being an outsider can make you a bit crap like that. She should know. None of this really spelled itself out in her brain you understand, but her toe grasped it, in the way that bodies sometimes do get hold of things before minds manage to. Her toe edged its way away from her without her really noticing, crept along the step, pulled her round a fraction, felt its way along the stone, and stubbed itself conspiratorily against Giddy's foot.

Giddy looked up sharply. Stick was a little taken aback by her foot's rash behaviour. 'It's nothing.' She managed finally, 'You know. This. They're just like this. They're always like this. Sort of. It's just, you know, for fun.' Stick's eyes were flat as she spoke. They stayed flatly and emptily on Giddy's for a moment and then she shrugged and turned them back on her reclaimed toe. But Giddy's foot had understood. He half smiled and shrugged along with Stick.

'I don't know why you hang around with them.'

'What do you mean "them"?' suddenly Stick's eyes were no longer flat, but skittery with suspicion and defence.

'Well, don't you have any friends your own age?'

'What do you mean "my own age"?'

'You know. Younger than them.' Giddy nodded back at the self-satisfied hut.

'I don't like hanging round with children,' Stick's tongue curled round the word as if it had decomposed in her mouth, 'if that's what you mean. Playing with their Barbies and feeding their baby dollies and listening to Stepz. Anyway I'll be thirteen next year and it will all be different.'

'What will?'

'Everything, dickhead.'

Giddy wasn't quite sure of his ground here. Obviously he knew girls changed in their teens but he wasn't too sure on the details of when, where, how. Did it all happen at once at thirteen? The big deal for him had been double figures. He didn't have that much pinned on thirteen. In Zelda your character got to be a teenager after you'd done a load of things and then you were on a higher level and got to kill Ganaderolf and rescue the princess and get your sword and that. And sure he'd like to get older and do what he wanted (like not come here for starters) and buy his own sweets. But he wasn't that specific about everything changing at thirteen. No he didn't have much pinned on that as such. But then he wasn't a girl. Though he couldn't quite be sure if this was a 'girl' thing or just a 'Stick' thing. A slightly disturbing image flitted through his head of Stick with legs and heels and tits.

'I'll be thirteen too next year,' he offered.

'So? You'll still be a wanker.' The image exploded. And so did Giddy.

'You're just stupid. So bldy stupid that you hang round with even stupider girls who are older than you. Who don't even like you. Who are horrible to you. Who you can't even stand up to. What's so great about them in their stupid hut? They chucked you out anyway. I don't care if you think I'm a wanker. I don't care if you all do. You think you're so great because you swear. Well you're not great at all. I've got my own friends at home. You don't. You don't have any real friends. You're just totally, utterly, completely the bldy stupidest stupid stupid around.'

The reply came screaming back at him.

'So? What do you know? eh? What do you know? What do you

know about anything? You're just a fucking kid, FUCKBRAIN.' And Stick fled Giddy, fled the precious beach-hut with its Holy Grail of chocolate and powder and raced down the steps to the sea.

Stick sat on the wet sand and scrabbled at the stones with spiky fingers and toes. Her eyes were set hard refusing space to any wimpy tears. She stared viciously at the waves. It was cold and windy still. But she didn't care. Not her fault she was the youngest. Not her fault she didn't fit in. Not her fault they'd shut her out. Not her fault she didn't like Barbie. (Anyway Kay pulled the head off her Hair-dressing Barbie and made her Wedding Barbie do rude things with Ken.) And why should she hang around with crap boys her own age who didn't know anything? Jan's brother could drive nearly. So there. And he'd taken time to play table tennis with her and chat to her properly like a grown up and not like Kay and Maz's little sister. So there. And soon she'd be a teenager and it would all be alright and she wouldn't be anyone's little sister any more. So there. So there. So there. Stick hurled stones into the sea, with every 'so'. She yanked her arm nearly out of its socket as she hurled them but she didn't care.

Gideon alone on the steps again watched the bundled up form of the small spikey boy-girl thing savage the sea with stones. Just him and the hut again – but now the growing chatter from inside it suggested warm possibilities of change. Anger still rattled round his ribs. Let Stick freeze on the beach. He'd have the hut to himself any minute now. He watched her spindly arm lashing out from her towel and the sea fizzing under the rapid hail of her stones . . . Not bad at throwing . . . For a girl.

Plop. A stone whizzed past and dropped into the sea by Stick. She didn't look round. It was that Giddy and there was no way she was going to talk to him any more. Fat lot of thanks she got for standing up for him. Not her fault she didn't belong. Not her fault. Not her fault. She flung out another stone and again another one whizzed past and plopped in next to hers. She hurled the next one with all her strength and the answering stone dropped just short.

'Ha,' she thought. 'Can't even throw stones. What sort of pathetic boy is that?' But even as she thought it a low flung stone took her by surprise. It skidded over the incoming wave and skimmed the trough beyond bouncing two, three, four, times before succumbing to the swell. Stick still didn't look behind her. Her fingers closed on a round flat stone. She crooked her wrist and let fly – three bounces, four – FIVE. Beat that. But the answering stone made six, her next one four, his three, hers six, his an undefinable seven or more and now he was charging down onto the beach too and they were laughing and shouting and hurling stone after stone. Half-naked mad bony creatures with towels for cloaks leaping at the water's edge like demented frogs oblivious to the spitting rain – momentarily forgetful of their animosity. Entirely forgetful of the stuck-up hut.

Which, is, of course, when it opened.

Maz, Lou, Jan and Babs. They swaggered out jeaned, booted and hooded up, puffing on a shared fag, the hut door carelessly open to the world. But no Giddy or Stick repentant on the step, begging to crawl in. A slight re-grouping – but only slight. Maz, Lou, Jan and Babs, stamping their heels at the top of the steps, puffing on a shared fag pointing at the near-naked stone-throwers and laughing.

'Stick's got a boyfriend.'

'Oh so you're with Giddy now.'

'Giddy's her boyfriend.'

'Stick loves Giddy. Stick loves Giddy.'

Giddy looks for a moment. Continues throwing stones. But Stick is still now. She looks up at them with that flat look of hers. Arms hanging. Only her towel in motion, whipped up by the wind.

'Hut's free now.'

'Better not leave them on their own, who knows what they'll get up to.'

'Come on, Stick, come with us. Leave brain-dead boy behind. He can have the hut all to himself now.'

'Come on, we're going.'

'Put this on and come.' A jumper hurled on the sand at her feet. Stick motionless still. Arms hanging. Eyes empty. Towel flapping. Giddy ignoring them continues throwing stones.

Nothing for a minute or so. Maz, Lou, Jan and Babs stand about, scuffing their boot heels and handing round the fag. Stick just stands. A lot of watching goes on. The Girls watch Stick standing and watch Giddy throwing. Stick watches Giddy throwing and watches the Girls watching her. Giddy just watches the stones. Then Maz gets bored.

'Oh come on Stick. We're going. You can't hang round here in the cold. Put that on and come.'

Stick fires up.

'Not what you said before, is it? Didn't give a shit till now did you? Me being in the cold. You didn't give a shit.'

'Don't be juvenile, Stick.'

'Juvenile yourself.'

'And don't use words when you don't know what they mean. Come on. We're going. Come on. Let's go.'

'So? Go. Go on then. Go.'

Stick stands proud and defiant. As proud and defiant as you can be in nothing but your knickers with a towel flapping round your ears and your big, pig sister calling your bluff.

'You want to stay here with moron features?'

'He's alright.'

'Oh, "alright" now is he?'

'"Alright"she says! Get that: "Alright"!'

'Well, Giddy's her boyfriend now.'

'Stick loves Giddy. Stick loves Giddy.'

'D'you fancy her Gideon? Do you? Cause Stick fancies you, that's *patently obvious*!'

Stick fails to reply to this new attack from Maz's deadly arsenal of words. The gap is rapidly filled.

'Stick fancies Giddy. Giddy fancies Stick.'

Over and over and over backed by shrieking laughter. Stick stands firm in her knickers, undismayed by her gyrating towel, swallowing her humiliation in silent gulps.

Maz, Lou, Jan and Babs begin to shuffle off. Watching over their collective shoulder, they swagger up the tarmac slope and disappear over the green behind the huts, still tossing back jeers and incomprehensible taunts that are whisked away or obscured by great gusts of wind and gales of laughter.

Gideon and Stick alone now with the beach-hut – it's door flapping open, its warmth escaped to sea. Two small bare figures on a vast bare beach. The huge naked sea a grizzled grey furred by winds. A big empty sky full of drizzle.

Gideon still throws his stones. Stick still stands and swallows. Dumped into a partnership by others, neither can look round. 'Stick loves Giddy' hangs above them. 'D'you fancy her?' hovers close: the frail alliance sagging under their too heavy weight. Necessity vanishing with the enemy. Nakedness bearing down.

Giddy's last stone spins. He stops. He turns. That mouth of his half smiles at Stick. A rueful 'good for you and thank you' kind of smile. He doesn't know it but it is the most careful smile that anyone could muster for a Stick so brittle from rejection. But it doesn't do. What could? Her little face stares back pinched and tight.

'Don't think that makes me your friend. Don't think I did that for you or because of what you said or anything like that. Don't dare ever, ever think I like you. You're just a Boy. I hate Boys. They're crap. Completely, utterly and totally fucking, crapping, crap.'

And Stick ran straight into the beach-hut, banged the door and shut him out.

ANN JOLLY

Stone Soup

I know that girl's going to be trouble the moment she steps off the bus. Eighteen or nineteen she looks. Something familiar in the way she stands. And a strong tongue on her. I hear it engage before I see her.

'Where do I get something to eat round here?' Her English words, loud and bright, rise above clacking Swahili tongues as she comes towards the duka where I sit with Mama Edson. We've got a business, Mama Edson and I, a duka selling whatever we can grow – tomatoes, mangoes, rainy season fungus. We put the money aside for medicines and school fees and for when we get old – that's the money our husbands don't take to buy millet beer. The duka's on a good site, close to the bus stop and just across from the Hollywood Bar. Our village is half way between Mwanza and Bukoba and not far from the Lake so the bus stops here for people to get off and walk about, trade, catch up with what's going on around the district and pass on gossip from town.

Crispin Mokono used to sell soda and cigarettes from here until he was killed in a bus crash and we took his place. 'The beginning of wisdom is to get you a roof,' the proverb says, so that's what we did. We put up walls of woven banana palm and nailed a tin roof on to poles fixed to a table. The roof shades us from the egg-yolk sun.

In the early morning Mama Edson and I hoe and weed our shamba, plant and water the crops and pick whatever's ready. 'It's hard work being a woman,' my mama said when I was little, 'but a whole lot more interesting.' Later in the day, when the buses come through, we're at the duka. Depending on the season we cut up watermelon or pineapple and lay it out on a big round aluminium tray so people can buy one slice at a time. Oranges, mangoes and bananas are all sold singly. My youngest girl, Joyful, she puts the tray on her head and walks round the bus tempting those still in their seats, to buy our fruits. I've told her, 'make sure you get the money from the bus people before you pass a single piece through the window.'

That's how it is with me. Joyful is twelve now, the only child still at home and I'm more than fifty and a grandmother so there'll be no more babies. I'm not sorry. Eleven's enough though I was lucky, all born healthy and only two dying as kids. Malaria and polio. My girls tell me they're going to have three of four. That's all.

'Don't tell your husbands,' I say and show them the herb for making the tea that stops babies starting.

'Oh Mama,' they say, 'that didn't work for you. We're going to the hospital for something that does.'

'Well,' I say, 'don't go to the Mission Hospital. They tell you there it's God's Will if you get pregnant.'

What rubbish. It's your husband's will. But if you don't meet his needs then he'll end up going with a bar girl.

Lillyanna, my eldest girl, goes on the Swedish HIV Project in Mwanza to get condoms. That girl's got no shame. Her husband says he's allergic to rubber. So how's she going to get him to put them on I ask her. She'll refuse him unless he does, she tells me. Things are certainly changing. Nobody ever told me I could refuse my husband. He tells me that with a woman, a man is direct, blunt and brutal. If not, he loses his pride and depends on her. This is what I tell my sons. A man doesn't have to control his passions but he has to be in full control of the heart.

The bus girl comes up to our stall and points at the bananas, the small sweet ones.

'How much?' she asks.

Mama Edson tells her and the girl buys three. All the time I'm looking at her like I've seen her somewhere before. She's not black and she's not white. I think maybe she's from Zanzibar or Pemba or one of the other Arab Islands along the coast. Her skin is the colour of cinnamon and her hair is quite light but long and crinkly, flowing down her back in a wild tormented stream. She squats down in the spiky shade of a thorn tree, peels one of the bananas and eats it. She's wearing a yellow shirt, jeans – and sandals. Usually only us Africans wear those flip flops made from old car tyres. Maybe she is African, but her voice isn't. I am filling up with curiosity about her.

The bus engine clanks and bangs as it starts up. The driver pumps the horn to say he's leaving.

'It's going,' I say in English to the girl and nod towards the bus but she just smiles and says, 'I'm not.' She has plump purply lips and regular white teeth.

Why is she staying in our village? Not much happens round here. All my kids longed to get away. If I was younger and Joyful was married and off my hands maybe I would want to get away. But it's too late. That kind of longing got pushed down in having babies. Each time the cord was cut that child took a bit of my longing and made it their own. Besides I've got a home here – and a bit of land – as well as having the business with Mama Edson. What could I do in town to earn a living? And what would people say if I left my husband? That sort of news would be round the district in less time than it takes for rain to fill water jars in the wet season. But it would shake him up. He would have to get out of that chair and get a jembe in his hand and do some digging. And go for water, cook food, milk goats, feed the hens and wash his clothes. I laugh to myself how that would leave him.

'What makes you smile?' asks Mama Edson so I tell her I was thinking that if you take away just one thing, like a wife, everything else goes haywire.

She nods, 'and if you add just one thing, like a child, it all goes haywire.'

I see that too.

Mama Edson and I have known one another since before we were born. Our mothers were expecting us at the same time and we lived side by side in this village. So we're like sisters. Together we learned to pound maize, balance water pails on our heads, grow rice and gut fish. And we got married to brothers around the same time so there isn't much we don't know about each other. Her name was Mary then but it's the custom for a woman to take the name of her first born son. Just like I was Angelica but now I'm Mama Julius. Even my husband calls me Mama Julius. Sometimes I forget that I have ever been Angelica.

Dry season dust the colour of chillies swirls about as the bus leaves and Mama Edson and I cover the stall with an old Kanga to keep off the dirt and the flies. The bus girl wipes her hands on her jeans and stands up. The men on the porch of the Hollywood Bar, our husbands among them, sit up in their chairs to watch the ripeness of her. She stretches, wriggles her legs out straight and tugs her jeans down. Then she comes back to Mama Edson and me at our stall, and asks in that loud English voice of hers:

'Excuse me, can you tell me where I can get a room round here?'

'There's only the Hollywood Bar,' we tell her pointing towards the men sitting with beer bottles in front of them.

She says 'thank you', and walks up the wooden steps between the men who haven't seen anything like her lushness since the year the rainy season lasted three weeks longer than usual. That evening I learn Johnston, who runs the Hollywood Bar and drinks its profits, has rented her a room in the concrete block out the back that the bar girls use. She doesn't look like a bar girl. My husband tells me she speaks kitchen Swahili – it's how they speak over the border in Kenya. Maybe she's from there. But why come here?

Later I hear word the bus girl's name is Daisy and that she's looking for someone. She does this looking at the bar – talking to people, drinking tea or having a few beers. In spite of her juicy look, there's something in her that makes me think she's thirsty, like land in a desert. A desert can have a strange effect on a person. As long as you search for outward things like underground water and new grazing for cattle, all is well. But if an inward longing wakes up, life wobbles, like a goat skittering on a pile of stones. I think Daisy has an inward longing. She has a sharp daring look of indifference too, and deep down inside me, where I don't usually go, I glimpse a longing like the one in Daisy. It frightens me that we might be kin in this way. A strange obsession with the bus girl is creeping into my life.

Two days after Daisy gets off the bus I sit at our duka picking stones from a tray of rice. She steps down from the veranda of the Hollywood Bar and comes towards me. The overhead sun casts a short fat shadow.

'Mama Julius,' she says in English, 'may I talk with you?'

'Be seated,' I say in Swahili. My English is small and I will not pretend she doesn't understand my language.

She sits beside me. Scarcely a breath of wind disturbs the stillness of the day and the spinach is bright green on the shaded table.

She wants to tell me her story. I listen.

'My mother is English but lived in Nairobi since before I was born. She worked for an aid agency based there when the drought was happening in Ethiopia. But in her time off she travelled through Kenya, Tanzania and Uganda. The borders were closed then but that didn't bother her. It was easy to avoid the patrols if she stayed off the main roads.'

'And your father?' I want to say but don't. When Daisy speaks again she answers the question I haven't asked.

'She got pregnant with me on one of those trips but I never knew who my father was. She mentioned him a little when my stepfather wasn't there but he didn't like hearing her talking about my real father. Though she already had me when she married him I think I'm one of the reasons they got divorced.'

Divorce. Daisy's world is shockingly apart from mine.

'But they rubbed along together until he was sent back to the UK with his company. My mother didn't want to leave Nairobi. She and I belonged in Africa, she said.'

'Did your mother have no other kids?' I ask.

Daisy shakes her head and I pity this mother of hers. Adrift with her only kid in a place far away from family.

'I was fourteen when he left and for the next four years or so my mother lived with friends and worked wherever she could. My stepfather sent her money. He wasn't a bad man. Just not my father.'

Why is Daisy telling me this?

'She earned enough to keep me at school and pay rent. There wasn't a lot of money but we survived.'

Daisy is so pulled into what she is saying that she forgets I am here. We sit on a crate padded with plastic seed sacks and her words and tears tumble out.

'At the start of this year my mother fell ill, very ill, though at first I thought it was nothing. She had never been ill before. Not really ill like this.'

I see the loneliness welling up in Daisy and lay my hand on her arm. Under the sleeve of her shirt she feels young and plump. She goes on.

'Cancer. She was in hospital. Then she died. Her friends helped me bury her.'

The words are spare and bone-dry.

'So what am I to do? The family we were living with are very kind. They say I can stay with them as long as I need. But I'm not a child. In England there is only my grandfather. I haven't seen him since I was ten and I've never lived there. He is old and has to be looked after. Friends of my mother's offer me jobs but I have no training. Despite all the people around me I do not belong anywhere, do not really know who I am.'

This is the thirst I sensed in Daisy. A different thirst from mine though the feeling of it is alike. Poor Daisy. For all her youth and those hips that sway like wind blown grass, she has nowhere on this earth that she can rightfully call her own. She goes on.

'When she knew she was dying my mother told me about my father, his name, the village where she met him and she said that I should search for him. Perhaps she thought he might look after me when she was no longer there.'

Suddenly I understand. 'No,' I scream inside. I could destroy her with the thunderbolt of violence within me. She turns towards me. Deceitful stranger, she has put on the mask of adaptability, assumed ways and manners that open doors and now I must listen to her words devouring my life.

'Mama Julius, I have found my father. But he is also your husband.'

Her sharp voice is filled with happiness. I do not move, just allow the grains of rice on the tray in front of me to trickle through my fingers.

'What makes you so sure?' My voice is cold and crackling like snakeskin. Inside I seethe and froth.

When she speaks, her words have the shape of truth and I have to believe her.

I didn't think my husband was faithful to me. I didn't expect it. I'm not that stupid. My mother taught me to know marriage for what it is. She beat me as a kid to prepare me for my husband's beatings. She was right. From the beginning, my married life was tainted with bruises and betrayals. Later when sons were born and my husband saw I was a good mother and a hard worker the beatings got less. As years went by and he grew older, a measure of peace has come between us.

So when matters of the flesh are almost past, it is very painful to have this half and half girl sit beside me, her face full of a delight that comes from the depths of my husband's passion with another woman. I had thought I was too old for the rage that floods me.

Then I see my husband ease his deceiving bones from his chair in the corner of the Hollywood Bar. He comes over. Half of him looks ashamed – that's the half that's married to me – and the other half, a much bigger half, looks pleased with himself as though planting a seed in a woman makes him a big potato.

'What a man,' his friends will say in admiration,

and

'What a man,' I say to myself. I dare not say it aloud.

'This girl is my daughter,' he says, 'You are my wife and I have told her to come and stay in my house. It is not right that a daughter of mine should stay where bar girls work.'

He returns to his cronies and Daisy's eyes are grains of light fluttering with hope. Dates and figures dance in my head. This girl was conceived when William was in hospital in Mwanza. Two years old my son was when he died of polio. His brother Juma was sick too but came home alive, though one of his legs will always be twisted and soft, like maize porridge. He hobbles with a crutch but is a clerk in the Nyanza Cotton Corporation.

'You don't have to run to keep accounts,' he says.

Now I learn that while I was nursing Juma and digging William's grave, their father was with this girl's mother. And he expects me to take her into our house and treat her as a daughter.

Later I sit with Mama Edson at our duka. The long rains are only weeks away and full bellied black clouds gather over the Lake to the north. Clouds also fill my heart. Mama Edson and I wait for the bus to come through. Already she knows that Daisy is my husband's kid for he cannot keep this proud news to himself.

'So you have a light skinned daughter,' Mama Edson says as we slice melon. The more pieces from each melon, the more profit, but if portions are too thin people will buy elsewhere. We know exactly how thick to make each bit.

I nod. The flames inside me are dying down. A coldness is taking their place.

'What will you do?' she asks.

I shrug. I will do as always. I will bear it.

'I wonder,' says Mama Edson, bony fingers laying out the melon in a sunburst on the tray, 'If your husband realises that she will have been brought up differently from our daughters.'

My home, where Daisy will live with us, is on the edge of the village. Built of mud and cement bricks, the roof is corrugated iron but there is no electricity. Life is tough here, no TV, no hamburgers, no water from a tap. We eat a little boiled meat or fish and maize porridge, some fruits and vegetables. There are foam mattresses for our wooden beds, but Daisy's life in Nairobi must have been very different.

'I know all this,' Daisy says when I tell her, 'but I still want to live in my father's house. And you must not treat me like a guest. I want to help, please treat me as a member of your family.'

I am very angry. She is not my family but what else can I do? My husband says she is to live with us so it happens. I explain her to Joyful who rolls her eyes but quickly becomes fascinated by Daisy with her chatter and laughter.

Months go by. I learn to tolerate Daisy's presence in my house and Joyful has fallen in love with this half sister, the girl woman with rolling buttocks and resonant voice. They sit in the doorway on a box with 'Handle Carefully' stencilled on it in big white letters. Daisy wears a yellow dress patterned with red fish swimming through blues lines of water and holds Joyful's hand in hers. Both palms are pink but Joyful's hand is black and bony, Daisy's is brown and fleshy. They are painting one another's fingernails with Daisy's pearly red varnish, whispering and giggling as they do so.

'Fetch water,' I shout, knowing there is no reason for a loud voice, except that my heart is angry. They stand up and swing the water pail between them as they go to the well.

Now that Daisy shares a room in our house with Joyful, my husband takes little notice. It is enough that she is under his roof. He relies on me to run the house and spends his time, as always, gossiping in the Hollywood Bar where men talk of politics, corruption and bride prices.

I treat Daisy as if she was a daughter of my house. I say, 'Make tea. Crush ginger on the edge of the step with a panga. Add it to the water boiling in the kettle. If rats run across the yard stamp on them, yes even if you have bare feet. This is how you add the tea, not so much. Add sugar. More. Keep your knees together or men will think you are easy. Strain the tea through a cloth into the green thermos. Screw the lid on tight. Tight, I said.

'Make ground nut paste. Roll roasted nuts and salt on that tin tray. With a beer bottle of course. Roll hard. Harder.

'Cook ugali. Light the charcoal with a hot ember. Well, run and get one from next door. Balance the water pail on a pad twisted from a cloth on your head. Your back must be straight. Don't hang around the well too long, people will talk. Use an enamel plate to fan the flames. Boil water in the big sufuria. Add the maize. Smoothly. Keep stirring. Serve the men first. You always come last.

'This is how you wash clothes. Use Omo, yellow soap is for floors, ash is for the plates. Don't hang around the Hollywood Bar or people will say a loose woman lives in this house. Toss rice in the air to lose the husks. Pick it over to find the stones. This is how you smile and say yes when you mean no. Johnston from the Hollywood Bar is bad news. This is how you smile and say no when you mean yes.'

Daisy listens, tries to please and laughs when she gets it wrong. She makes a good imitation of a dutiful daughter. I acknowledge she is a hard worker – and a hard talker too. Daisy talks of men and babies and sex with a vigorous relish I have not heard before, not even from my own daughters who have been to school and are married with families of their own. Women have always talked of these things but Daisy speaks also of university education for women, computers, the role of the World Bank in the debts of developing countries, the way women's work is unvalued, the state of the world. My head spins with trying to understand what she is saying. Our conversations get tangled up and the African night creeps all about us. Kerosene lamps are lit, the conversation gets more intense and when my husband returns home for food it is not always ready. I am dazed by Daisy and her waterfall of words and ideas and thoughts and her loud ringing, sprawling laughter.

'Where is my food?' my husband shouts.

'We were talking,' Daisy says, 'sit down Baba and wait for it to cook.'

And he does.

I am timid and subdued in the face of my husband, of authority. Anything can overwhelm me. Not because I like it like this but because authority carries the weight of ages pressing down on my life. Daisy does not know this feeling. She has opinions to spare, can shout and disagree and argue, knowing her world will not crash around her if she does. She is oddly beautiful with a big strong stride in our narrow constricted world – as if the cross currents of Africa and Europe have blended in harmony within her. Although she is young and without a mother she makes me feel I am the kid, the one with things to learn. Joyful is attracted by her vivid, wayward thoughts and eagerly listens to our discussion as we work and drinks spicy tea with us when we rest. Then Mama Edson and other women drift towards us and sometimes as many as seven or eight of us muse on concerns of love or the position of women. This joining together of women to talk of outside things is new and powerful. The men in the Hollywood Bar shift in their chairs and look uneasy when they see us. The rage I feel towards Daisy dwindles, though when my husband says, 'that daughter of mine has grown into a fine woman,' it flares up again. But it points in a different direction.

Daisy is leaving, going back to Nairobi. She is wearing her jeans and the African car tyre sandals. We stand at the bus stop just before dawn. The dark blue sky is filled up with bright specks of stars that speak of mystery. Joyful cries and I give Daisy the best fruits from our shamba tied in a cloth to eat on her journey.

'Mama Julius,' she says and throws her arms around me. 'I will come back and see you. And you must come and visit me in Nairobi with Joyful.'

'And you too Baba.' she says to my husband as they shake hands. I suspect he is secretly glad he will no longer be confronted by this bothersome daughter with her raucous laughter and wild challenges to tradition.

I am mixed up. I hated her at first for who she was but when I know her for herself I see differently. Through Daisy blows the rushing wind of freedom, conferring on me, as it passes, that same licence to think and question. Daisy is not frightened. She may be dejected or lonely but she is not scared or faint hearted. I am so afraid and afraid is not alive.

The bus appears through the darkness, rumbling and jangling. Out jumps the conductor to put a stone under the back wheel so the bus won't roll away. He and the driver drink early morning tea from tin flasks. Daisy climbs aboard and fights for a seat. The last I see of her is a plump brown hand waving through the window as the bus changes gear where the road turns at the end of the village.

Daisy is like the wandering traveller who makes stone soup. This traveller comes to a small village where everyone is hungry. No one has enough to eat and each person hoards what little she has. People fear outsiders. One day the traveller begins boiling water in a huge pot to which she adds very large stones, one by one. A village woman stares for a long time as she stirs the mixture. Finally she asks, 'What are you doing?'

'I'm making stone soup,' the traveller replies, 'but something is still missing. Perhaps you would like to try some?'

The villager tastes the soup and agrees. Something is missing.

'Maybe I could bring a few carrots for it?' she suggests.

Other women come. Each sees what the traveller is doing, each asks about the curious broth brewed from stones and each offers to bring a little of what they can spare. One brings a few potatoes, another an onion, a third a cabbage and soon there is a variety of rich ingredients in the sufuria.

As the women gather around the soup pot, telling each other stories they feel part of a celebration. The soup is delicious and there is enough for all. They are nourished, not just by the tempting food, but by the working together that has made it possible.

And they say, 'We need never go hungry again now we know how to make soup from stones.'

I walk some steps behind my husband. He chooses not to see how Daisy has affected me with her extravagant words. I am a clear stream emerging from dark decaying undergrowth. I hold Joyful's hand as we go towards our house and I think maybe Daisy has shown me how to make stone soup. I hope I have not come too late to the feast.

SIMON BACK

Billy Brown of London Town and the Troglodytes of Bow

Down below the station's bright
But here outside it's black as night
Billy Brown will wait a bit
And let his eyes get used to it
Then he'll scan the road and see
Before he crosses, if it's free;
Remembering when lights are dim
That cars he sees may not see him

Our father refused to allow us to be evacuated. 'We shan't be bombed,' he insisted. 'And if we are, we'll all die together, at home.' He worked in the docks in a bond warehouse. It was one of the first to get hit when the Germans started their raids and he and some friends dug through the rubble to recover as much stuff as they could, selling it on to black marketeers up West. Father was a proud man, a stoical man, and he did what he had to do to get by and provide for us all. I never saw him cry but I never heard him laugh either.

Our mother was completely the opposite, quite dippy in a dependable way and always concerned with her appearance. I remember watching her, bemused, drawing a line up her calf before she went to 'The Feathers' with Father. 'Makes me look like I've got stockings on,' she said. 'Makes me feel special.' She knew little of the machinations of the world and questioned nothing, which made it all the more surprising when she argued with Father over what should be done about my sisters and me. I think she was probably panicking. Everyday she saw the posters – 'Mothers – evacuate your children' or some such and she helped her friends pack their kids off to Bethnal Green where they were forwarded to God knows where in the country. After that August bank holiday when they moved everyone out of the cities I heard her crying in the night and then heard Father get out of bed and stomp downstairs. She always gave in to his will though. It must have been easier for her.

When the bombs came mother huddled us all in a corner and read to us, usually 'Biggles and the Something or Other', by the light of a single candle. Father sat by the fire which smoked the room out because the wood was always wet. He read the paper over and over and burned a lamp he had 'liberated' from the docks. 'Jerry shan't see it through my curtains,' he said, victoriously. He had put them up himself within hours of the Blackout being declared. It was his way of covering up for his earlier assertion that there would be no Germans bombing Bow.

But the Germans did come, and relentlessly. Father locked the door when the sirens sounded and we endured the distant sound of explosions and the not-so-distant sound of fire engines speeding through the pitch-black streets. In the morning, he would unlock the door at the sound of the all-clear and we would step out under the fire-lit heavens and later, when the sun rose, we would look at the burned out buildings and the collapsed houses and wonder what it was all about.

Most people in our street took shelter underground. There were plenty of places to hide: cellars under pubs, crypts under churches, various tunnels between here and there, underground warehouses and, of course, the Tube. Mother begged Father to take us to one of these places but he refused. 'We're safe enough here,' he said and wouldn't be persuaded otherwise. He recounted tales told him at work, that cellars were cold and damp and rat infested, that crypts were full of rotting corpses and ghosts who didn't like company. The tunnels were nothing but sewers, he said, and the warehouses full of disease and 'Nig Nogs', by which he meant Asian and African folk. He admired them and their desire to work hard but he was always suspicious of them, too.

He never had time for the Tube, even before the war, and always went by bus in case he 'missed something'. I had grown up with tales of the Troglodytes of Bow, a race of small, black, hairy people who lived in the tunnels of the Metropolitan Line and scavenged about the tracks and sewers. Sometimes they grabbed children off the platforms and pulled them down into their ever-dark world and made you into one of them. But if they didn't like you, they fried you in lard and ate you bit by bit. He gave lurid eyewitness reports, which he read out of the paper, from train drivers and engineers who had seen the creatures in their own environment, skulking in the stinking labyrinth and stealing food and equipment from them. Sometimes they would be bedazzled by the lights of an oncoming train and get splattered across the front of it and women in the next station would faint at the sight. Other times, the 'folk downstairs' or 'them in the earth' as they were called, would fall onto the live track and be fried to a crisp. That's when the trains got delayed – Troglodyte on the tracks. He said they had a whole city down there, with houses and factories and shops selling stuff stolen from above and that they never, ever came up in daylight because the sun would kill them as surely as the electric tracks. If they had a city, I reckoned, they couldn't be all that bad. Father smacked me on the ear and reminded me that the Germans had cities, too, and was I saying *they* weren't all that bad? Like Mother, I gave in.

Those stories put the fear of God in my sisters and me. Mother said he was making it up but she said it in a way that left me with the impression that she wasn't so sure, which just made it seem all the more true. When the bombs came, father added a new string to his anti-Tube bow. He wasn't going to pay London Transport for a ticket and not go anywhere because you had to pay 1½d to be allowed onto the platform and sheltering there was, in any case, discouraged on safety grounds. Given the choice between being bombed, crushed and burned alive though, many decided to risk the slim chance of falling onto the track or, indeed, of abduction by the Troglodytes.

One morning we got up after a raid and found the Jones's house over the road was not there any more. There was just a bath sticking out of the wall at a right angle. The Joneses had been so proud of that bath. We had a tin bath that we kept in the yard. 'I hope there was no one in it,' Mother said, before bursting into tears.

That night, when the sirens sounded, Mother took my sisters and me out to the tube station. She completely ignored Father for the first time in her life. He swore and stayed in the house as Mother slammed the door behind her. I looked to see if he was watching us through the window, but he wasn't. It was pitch black and we were nearly run down by a car. We heard it coming but didn't see it until the last minute and he was going too fast to really see us. They weren't allowed to switch their headlights on, you see, what with the blackout and all. They were a bit paranoid about light guiding the Junkers and the Heinkles – even the pubs had to have light traps behind the doors if they were going to be open.

I'd only been down into the station once before, a couple of years ago, just to see what it was like. Father told me off for trespassing when I told him and that kept me away afterwards. It therefore all looked new to me. We joined the queue for platform tickets. More and more were joining the lines all the time. We stood by a poster featuring a smug little man in pinstripes and a bowler. His name was Billy Brown of London Town and he was supposed to advise people on the correct use of the Underground through insufferable verse. I'd heard of him in passing – jokes in the street – that sort of thing, but I'd never thought people hated him until I saw this poster. It read: 'He never jostles in a queue / but waits his turn. Do you?' To which some wit had added with a pencil: 'You annoy so much, you really do / I wish you dead. Do You?' Through the cracks between people I saw one or two others plastered about. One looked like it was about to fall off the wall and was flapping in the breeze.

There was a warden trying to direct people and check tickets. He kept getting into arguments with people who had no tickets and that slowed the lines down even further. Then I recall there was this sudden surge from behind and I was crushed up against a man in a tweed jacket. My youngest sister was pushed to the floor and nearly trampled to death in the stampede. The warden was sent spinning out of the way as hysteria washed through the crowd and they ran for the escalators. I was separated from Mother and my sisters and spent ages and ages being jostled and kicked and trodden on. Then there came a familiar booming sound and everyone on the platform fell silent. The sky was falling again, but we were safe down here.

I found my sisters eventually, huddled along the far end of the platform next to the tunnel entrance. They were sharing a bread bun. I asked them where they had got it and they pointed to an odd looking fellow a few feet away. He was sat on a stool with a crowd around him. He seemed to be doing magic tricks. He was only as tall as me and had a humpback. At first I wondered who he was, wondered if perhaps he was a Troglodyte, then I realised he must be 'Henry'. I heard about 'Henry the Magic Dwarf' from my friends but he was certainly a weird looking chap.

'Where's Mum?' I asked my sisters. They just stared. I asked them again and they burst out crying. 'Where is she?' I shouted. Henry looked up from his enthralled audience and waddled over to us.

'You the bruvva, eh?' he said. I nodded. 'Yer Muvva's up top wiv the uvva's.' He patted me on the head, said he'd see us all right, and went back to his audience.

I calmed my sisters down and sat there with them in silence. Mum had probably seen us safe and gone back home to be with Father. That would be just like her. There was a murmur of conversation along the platform and some laughter from Henry's show. Someone started playing a harmonica but was cut short by someone who threw it onto the tracks with a clatter. The station was the most boring place I'd ever been.

A boy came along. I say a boy, but he was probably about sixteen. He started chatting, asked us where we lived, why we hadn't been evacuated. He kept looking around us, as if he'd lost something.

'Did you hear? About the crush?' he said.

'What crush?'

'Up top. Too many trying to get in. There's loads got killed.'

I was a bit shocked. 'I think we got away before that happened. I hadn't heard . . .' Then I thought of Mother and fell silent.

Henry shouted over towards us. He called the boy 'Danny' and told him to leave us be.

Danny just sneered and said to me: 'How many swear words d'you know?'

'I don't know any.'

'Ah, you do, come on. D'you know . . . "damn"?'

'Yes, of course.'

'What about . . . "bloody"?'

I looked about nervously, felt my face flushing. Henry was waddling towards us, stepping over sleeping people as well as he could. 'Please don't . . .' I said glancing down at my sisters who were practically asleep. Father did not allow swearing in the house unless he was the one doing it.

'I know,' the boy said. '"Fuck". Can you say "fuck"?'

'No. I'd like to go to sleep now, please.'

'Ah, go on. I'll give you sixpence. Say it. Say "fuck off".'

Tempting as it was, I never did. He caught sight of Henry coming towards us and made off. He was up to something, I knew, but it wasn't that which scared me. What really put the willies up me was what he said as he went away. He said: 'Suit yourself. I'd watch out for the Troglodytes though, if I were you. This close to the tunnel – they only have to reach out and grab your leg and they'll be off with you. Wouldn't catch me falling asleep down 'ere.'

'You all right?' Henry asked.

I nodded.

'You watch 'im. Nasty piece o' work. Get yourself some nod, y'ere?'

As it was, I didn't get much sleep in the end. Time and again I thought I heard a noise like a Troglodyte, but there was nothing there, or I thought one was gripping my ankle, but it was my sister's foot. The air on the platform was warm from the hundreds of bodies piled up there like sand bags and it smelled of piss. People used the tracks as a sewer since they had to use somewhere. The wardens warned against it but short of building a toilet block, there was nothing they could do. People bought a bucket and then tipped it over the side. Some of the men just peed straight onto the rails. A horror story reached me during a wide awake period that night telling how a man had peed onto the live rail and the electricity had been conducted by the pee right back to him and frazzled him. It was probably rubbish, but I considered it along with the frazzled Troglodytes and it became less and less apocryphal.

In the morning everyone filed out in an orderly fashion. There were a lot of police about and the street was full of ambulances. They were carrying people out, and I realised that the boy must have been telling the truth. I asked a policeman. He told me to run along home. I heard other grown-ups talking about seventy people dead in the crush. I hustled my sisters through the crowds and into the street. Mother was nowhere to be seen, so she *must* have gone home. The sun was shining and it looked like all the bombs had missed Bow altogether. There wasn't a scratch on any of the buildings. Then I suddenly felt sorry for whoever *had* been hit. When we came round the corner to our street, it was gone. Our house and the others around it were gone, replaced with piles of brick and stone and wood and roof slate and belongings. The only thing that still resembled a house was the Jones's place with the bath still sticking out of the wall. It hadn't been touched.

Our house was now just a heap of rubble with a doorstep and the bottom part of a window. Some shrapnel gatherers came by, looking for spoils, mementoes. They were a pain in the arse but the wardens tolerated them because they often found unexploded bombs and alerted the authorities. They saw us and retreated in guilty haste. Neither my sisters nor me felt much like crying. It wouldn't have changed anything. We sat on the step and waited for our parents to come home.

There seemed no point in blaming the Germans. I'd never met any and they didn't look any different to us on the newsreels. They were just an idea. It didn't seem like they really *existed.* People wouldn't do this sort of thing. No, I decided, it was the bombers that had done this. The planes. Considering the reactions I had seen others display to news of loss and death, I felt strangely forgiving. I was too young to understand what the war was about and so were my sisters. All this destruction was just normal to us, like wind and rain and sun. Sometimes the Germans bombed us. Sometimes we bombed them, so it couldn't be wrong, could it? If we were doing it, I mean? We were British, we lived in a kingdom, had an empire. We had power and glory and God was on our side.

I explained all this to the warden who found us and took us to the church hall, which had escaped night after night of bombing. He said I sounded like a right little Hitler. I don't know what he meant exactly. Hitler was not a nice man, that's about all I knew. The warden introduced us to Henry the Magic Dwarf. I told him we'd already met. The warden said good, and that Henry would sort us out. I wish he hadn't bothered.

It seems Henry was a bit of an activist in the community. He had run a shelter in an old underground stable in Stepney until the wardens had taken over and pushed him out. He had gone around organising others since. Last night he ended up sorting out ours. I asked him how many people had died.

'One or two,' he said. 'Often 'appens. People git excited.'

He handed us all a teacake and told us to settle down somewhere. A tall man, three times Henry's size, slapped him on the back as we ripped off the first handfuls of bread and stuffed them into our mouths. He was dressed in rags and looked like he had never washed.

'Henry, you short arsed commie, how you doing?' he said.

'Lofty, y'old scrounga. Fought you'd 'ad yer 'ead knocked off by an 'einkle.'

'What's the weather like down there?' the man called Lofty responded.

They went on like this for sometime, trading insults, slapping and punching each other. They were an odd couple. Then Lofty said:

'Heard you were spending the night at the Pally.'

'Time to kick the decadent bastards where it 'urts. They can't stop us.'

'Grand. Count me in.'

'You'll lose yer 'ead dahn there. Better lose a few feet.'

'Only got the two, Hen, you know that. Need both of them to stand up, like.'

I was staring at the size of the man's feet. Never had seen such slabs. Neither had I ever seen shoes that size in any shop.

'What are you looking at, boy?' Lofty said. It took me a moment to realise he was talking to me.

'Nothing, sir.'

'Well piss off then and stop hanging about like flies round shit.'

I took my sisters to the end of the church hall and sat down next to a young man in a uniform. He had an eye missing. He didn't try to cover it up. He wore it as proudly as he wore his uniform. My elder sister kept asking what had happened to him. I kept telling her to shut up and stop being so rude. Eventually, she asked him herself. He told us all about Dunkirk and about how he had been blown into the water when a Stuka hit the rescue boat he was on. He had been pulled out by another boat that was already overloaded and really low in the water because of it. Then I told him what had happened to us and I told him about the man who pissed on the line and the Troglodytes.

'Well, I don't know about peeing on the line, but the Troglodytes are real enough,' he said.

'Have you seen one?' I said excitedly.

'Oh, sure. Don't believe everything they say about them. They don't eat people.'

'Don't they?'

'Would you go to all the trouble to kidnapping something as big as a human when you've got millions of rats to pick from? Of course not.'

'They eat rats?'

'Sure, just like the French eat frogs and horses.'

'I think you're pulling my leg, sir. The French don't eat frogs and horses.'

'They did when I was in Paris.'

'You were in Paris?'

'Before we got pushed back to the coast, yes.'

He went on for hours about the war and Europe and places I'd never heard of that were being torn apart by tanks and aircraft. His stories excited me and I forgot the things I had been thinking before.

Henry gathered us up just before it got dark and declared that we were sheltering in luxury that night. He and Lofty led about a hundred people through the streets to a building called the Palais. I couldn't pronounce it at first but a woman told me it was said 'Pally' and I realised that this was the place Henry and Lofty had been discussing earlier. It was where Mother had always wanted to go and where Father had always refused to take her. 'What's wrong with The King's Arms?' he'd say. 'You don't want to worry yourself with poncy places like that. Full of poofs and hob nobs.' It was certainly a posh-looking place, even with the lights switched off.

Henry got into an argument with the doorman and cracked him across the knees with a crowbar. The doorman went down and Henry led us all inside. There was a big dome like the picture house had had before it got a direct hit, all gold and red and chandeliers. I didn't feel at all comfortable there. We went down some stairs to an underground ballroom all done out in mirrors and flowery carvings. There was a big polished dance floor with velvet seats round the outside. The chairs and tables had legs carved into lion's feet. There were sofas and silverware and napkins folded into funny shapes. Lofty welcomed everyone in and then began handing round cake. Not much cake, but cake it was. I hadn't seen any for nearly three years. It was the best thing in the world.

I settled my sisters down on a sofa and propped myself up against it to watch Henry perform his magic tricks with the air raid sirens for accompaniment. And then the roof caved in.

They pulled me out at about three o'clock the following afternoon. It was drizzling. I was in agony but nothing was broken, just cuts and bruises which they treated as best they could on overstretched resources. Then I found myself back at the church hall. I asked everyone who came in if they had found my sisters yet. Without fail, they all smiled and patted me on the head and assured me that they would turn up.

I sat there for two days, shivering, waiting, endlessly reading the graffiti poking fun at Herr Hitler and his mad friends. There was even a picture of Roosevelt with his head stuck in the ground and a bomb up his arse. That was my favourite. Sometimes I woke myself up talking to my sisters in my sleep, telling them it would be all right, that Mum was coming for us. In the end I went to look for my sisters myself. I couldn't walk very well. My knees were like jelly and my head pounded. The wardens were knocking down what remained of the Pally. I asked a warden if they had found two little girls in matching yellow dresses, about four and five years old.

'I've been here thirty-six hours straight, son.'

'Well, they're still in there, then.'

'Then they're dead.'

'They might not be.'

'Believe me, son, they will be.'

'But they can't be! I mean, they're my sisters! I was looking after them. I was all that was left! Mum and Dad!' The warden put his arms round me and my legs gave way. 'I'm the last one left.'

I woke in hospital on a makeshift bed in a corridor. People were rushing past right, left and centre, nurses, doctors, walking wounded and the dead on trolleys, their faces covered by white sheets stained so often that they no longer washed clean. I wished I were dead so that I too could have a sheet over my face so I did not have to look at the horrors around me. I only had tears to cover my eyes. Everything distorted and twisted as if the hospital was melting. It was an improvement.

It was really noisy. Everyone was talking at once, but I couldn't pick out any single words. I thought I heard my sisters at one point and thought I saw Mother with them, but it wasn't them. I was totally alone. Eventually somebody came by and spoke to me. He was tall and dark and wore a dog collar. I'd never seen a black vicar before. I didn't even know they were allowed to be vicars. He spoke to me but I can't remember a word he said. They were the first words I had heard in ages. He wiped away my tears with the corner of his handkerchief. He soothed me and only left when he had made me smile. I sat up to see where he had gone but he was lost to me in the torrent of people. Then I saw he had left a bright new sixpence by my pillow. Sixpence. And I hadn't had to say 'fuck'. Best not to have done, I suppose, him being a man of God and all. I looked at the coin again, turned it over in my hand. A really weird idea came to me, the answer to all my problems.

I ran through ruined, empty streets. Fires still burned and belched smoke into the sky. It seemed to me that the war would have to stop soon once there was nothing left to bomb. Then again, perhaps they would bomb the ruins. Even the tube station was battered. It was still open though and that was the point of my leaving the hospital. I told the man at the kiosk to keep the change.

It was something I had always wanted to say but never had enough money to do it. Now it didn't matter. I had the perfect answer to my trials. I would pee on the line. No. That occurred to me, but I wasn't sure someone my height would hit the live rail. No, I was going to join the Troglodytes.

Down on the platform I heard my sisters call my name. It took me by surprise, and I looked around. They weren't to be seen. I guessed I was still hallucinating. The man from Dunkirk had told me how he had heard voices when he came out of hospital. Then I heard my Father and I shook that off, too. It didn't even sound much like him to be honest. I stood right next to the tunnel and peered into the gloom. I could see about fifty feet, then it curved away. There was room to walk at the side of the rail, especially for a boy. The Troglodytes must be quite small, I remember thinking as I dropped down over the edge of the platform. I took a deep breath and a last look at the light and I stepped into the darkness. The voices called out to me, beckoning me. I passed the imaginary line where the light stopped. My eyes dilated and suddenly I could see much further. A rat scurried by, squeaking a warning that I was coming. It thought I was a hungry Troglodyte. I suppose I was. Unless there was some sort of joining ritual, I was already a Troglodyte, forever and ever. And I was definitely hungry. Rats would just be something I had to get used to.

My mother called my name. Her voice echoed around the tunnel and was swallowed by the dark. Ahead was a scratching sound and something rose up ahead. My mother shouted at the top of her ghostly voice.

'It's all right. I'm all right,' I called back.

The thing ahead had two glowing red eyes. It growled and shuffled its feet on the stony ground. A shiver ran down my spine and I wondered if it would eat me or befriend me.

My mother called my name again. I turned round instinctively, the words 'fuck off' forming on my lips. And there she was, silhouetted against the light.

'Where are you going?' she asked.

'To see the Troglodytes.'

'There are no Troglodytes you fool. Come out now! Right this minute.'

'We've followed you from the hospital,' said a man. He appeared behind my mother, his silhouette distorting hers. I couldn't see him, but I recognised his voice. It was the vicar from the hospital, calm and soothing as ever. 'I hope you haven't spent all that money I gave you.'

I gulped and glanced back at the creature, momentarily torn between two worlds. It shrank back as if letting me go. Its eyes continued to glow and I wished it well and walked back towards the light.

CHRIS POWELL

Burning the Blue-winged Boys

Sitting half way up the sloping field behind Sadie's house, they watched the funeral party swarm over the back garden, beetle-stiff, monochrome scraps stirring and turning like burnt litter across the grass. The air was rigid with the crawling feel of damp sheets and the field reeked of ancient cowpats and crushed nettles.

Many years later, when she had children of her own, Nancy revisited the field and felt again that sticky, thunder-bearing atmosphere. She was ten, and tired after a long journey south. Her cousins, Sadie and Esther, were both twelve and went to the same school; Esther was three months older than Sadie, which was important. Age generally seemed to matter a lot then.

'How will Gabriel cope?' People asked, 'He must be well into his seventies.'

'She was only sixty-seven,' they said, 'it's no age is it?'

To Nancy, Sadie and Esther sixty-seven was a very great age and although they were sorry their grandmother was dead and they composed their faces into suitable expressions of grief during the church service, she had always been old. As Sadie said, when a young person dies then that really is sad.

'Won't you miss her?' asked Nancy.

'I would have done,' said Sadie, 'when I was younger. When I used to stay with her and granddad a lot.' She snorted and paused to pull a lump of goose grass off her skirt, 'my dad just loves this sort of occasion. Mum had to stay up all night making those fucking sandwiches.' She glanced sideways at the other two. Nancy flinched. Esther giggled, her eyes bright with mischief. The word fucking hung between them like a neon sign. Sadie produced a small cylindrical cigarette lighter from somewhere and began flicking it on and off. She stabbed the flame at Nancy's face, 'what are you staring at?'

'How can he love his mother's funeral?'

Sadie held the lighter really close to Nancy's eyes. 'You are *such* a baby!' she said.

She could still see that tiny flame inside her eyelids for ages after Sadie stopped flicking it at her. It clung on to the edges of her nightmares longer than anything else about the afternoon of her grandmother's funeral, longer than granddad shouting; longer than the smell of burning hair or Aunty Muriel, Esther's mother, hissing at them to stop making the place look untidy and hand round some sandwiches, longer than Esther hiding the sandwiches on top of the cistern in the downstairs toilet, than heat and darkness and wanting to cough; grandma's creepy friend Mrs. Duckett tripping over a tub of mauve petunias, the flesh at the top of her leg slopping out of its stocking like cold porridge; a flash of livid colour exploding into the sky or the afternoon suddenly streaked with twilight and running, running across the fields to the old barn.

Nancy ran as fast as she could, but her cousins had longer legs and ran faster. They were both sitting astride the riding branch of the horse chestnut tree next to the barn when she caught up with them. The riding branch sprang from one of the main limbs. Thicker than a rugby player's flank, it swept down to within a couple of feet of the bare earth, its bark rubbed smooth and glossy by countless pairs of joy-riding legs. Pumping up from the ground you could make it buck and heave inexhaustibly and although the branch could easily bear the weight of two, or even three, girls, one alone could achieve the wildest, most riotous motion if her legs were strong enough. Esther once hung on for so long she made herself sick.

But now it swayed demurely under their weight. Sadie had whipped off her wrap-over skirt to reveal a pair of lime green shorts, she wore a black skinny-rib jumper, too hot for summer, and her hair was marbled gold by the sun through the leaves. Esther, sitting behind, had swung her legs up around Sadie's waist so that her bare feet rested on the branch between Sadie's thighs and her shift dress rode up around her hips; their faces were flushed with secrets, their white limbs whispered like spies in the shadows. Then Esther let her legs down and slid off the branch, jamming her feet back into her sandals as she landed. You could see the deep hemline where she had clumsily shortened her dress the night before, not leaving Aunty Muriel time to protest. Nancy still got dressed in whatever her mother put out for her, today it was her navy pleated school skirt and a pale blue blouse.

'Come on then,' said Esther. 'Before they start looking for us.'

She and Sadie headed towards the barn, leaving Sadie's skirt dangling carelessly from the branch. Nancy hung back, watching.

'How do you get in?' She wished desperately that her voice didn't sound so squeaky. Bales of straw packed methodically between the stone walls presented a sheer cliff face rising two thirds of the way up to the corrugated iron roof. She approached the barn and prodded the bales experimentally, testing for cracks and sink holes. 'Perhaps we could pull one out,' she suggested, trying to show willing.

Esther turned slowly, folded her arms across her chest. She looked like a sharp, raggedy black bird with her thin legs, narrow face and crumpled, unevenly hemmed shift. 'Very clever!' she said.

'Have you tried shifting one of these?' Sadie had her fingers slotted underneath a taut stretch of twine. 'Go on, try!' Nancy was about to give a placatory shake of her head, but Sadie's lip curled expectantly, challenging her. She sought out a bale that looked as if it might be less secure than the others. She squeezed her hands beneath the twine, one at each end of the bale so that her arms were extended to their full reach; ends of straw scraped her knuckles and her fingers turned white around the joints where they gripped the cords. She braced her legs against the base of the stack and leaned. Her knees ached with the strain, sweat snaked down the sides of her ribs, the twine sliced like cheese wire into her hands, and the bale didn't shift even one thousandth of an inch.

'See,' said Esther as Nancy pulled her raw, useless hands away. 'They do it all with machines.' Sadie looked at Nancy's damp blouse.

'Do you not use an anti-perspirant yet? Never mind. Let's stop wasting time. You see,' she bent down, whispering, 'We know where the secret entrance is. But before we allow you in, you have to promise.' She looked at Esther, who nodded gravely. 'You must promise you will never, ever, even if they threaten and torture you, let on about this place and what we do here. If you do tell, that'll be it. The end. Promise?' She gripped both of Nancy's wrists, hard, and stared into her eyes without blinking.

'I promise,' said Nancy, her eyes watering. 'Why?'

'Tell her, Es.'

'Because it's dangerous. Because they found out once and they've forbidden us. If they know we've come back again . . .' She drew a finger across her throat.

'Is it really dangerous?'

'A boy suffocated last year,' said Esther. Two pairs of expressionless eyes fixed on Nancy, daring her to chicken out. Then, with a simultaneous movement, they turned their faces to the wall of straw. Sadie went first. Expertly, she began to climb, finding toeholds, notches for her fingers, ascending effortlessly and swiftly. Esther's movements were spikier, more aggressive, but equally efficient. Nancy's feet slid off the treacherous straw and thudded into the cracked ground. It wasn't fair! Her knees were criss-crossed with little scratches, her socks were filthy and an angry rash was developing on her wrists. 'Ow!' she shouted, half-way between a sob of rage and cry of pain.

'Don't be such a baby!' Esther's head appeared, poking out of a narrow gap about ten feet up. She leaned further out and reached down a thin arm. Esther hauled, Nancy thrashed about, kicking up a whirlwind of dust-dry straw, and eventually landed on a narrow platform extending into the interior of the stack. Sadie stared at her with a look of profound boredom, looked to Esther briefly and, with a flick of her heels was gone, head first, her legs slithering into the darkness of a steep, tight tunnel between the bales of straw like one of those strange, luminous submarine creatures whose long trailing tails, flashing like neon ribbons, slip silently and swiftly under the rocks and vanish leaving the seabed bereft of light and colour.

'It's all right,' said Esther, 'but you have to keep going.' And she too disappeared.

The tunnel was just broad enough for a girl's shoulders to squeeze into and barely high enough to allow her head and buttocks to wriggle along. It was hot, prickly and profoundly dark. Nancy felt the stack of straw quaking above her head; one small realignment, one little shift of equilibrium and she would drown beneath the solid weight of straw, squashed flat like the moth she'd pressed between sheets of blotting paper inside her school atlas, her breath crumbling like sand as the bone-caressing silence slowly squeezed her dry. She thought about the boy who had suffocated. She could see nothing, hear nothing and she couldn't turn back. So she crawled forwards, wanting to scream but unable to because there wasn't enough air, her mouth was clogged with dust and anyway nobody knew she was there. The tunnel pursued a horizontal course for a few endless yards, then it dipped sharply downwards. She stopped crawling and fell, helplessly clawing at the straw as she slid headfirst and blind through the narrow channel and at last, after what seemed like hours, thudded on to a scratchy, sweltering plateau, gasping for air, her skirt ravelled up under her arms, her right shoe hanging off.

When her eyes became accustomed to the dim light, she saw Sadie sitting in a roughly circular depression in the centre of the stack. The bales here had suffered a landslip and slumped, broken-backed, in loose, indistinct heaps like melting chocolate. Nancy adjusted her clothing and began to calculate an escape route towards a tiny window just visible in the rear wall. Esther emerged out of the twilight with a square, battered biscuit tin under one arm. She carefully placed the tin on an intact bale. All three girls were silent. The air was a soup of dust, mites and floating straw, it smelled of mouse shit. A quick rustle from the darkness made Nancy sit bang upright; she badly needed to cough.

Outside, the clouds slid away from the sun. A pale bolt of light shot through the window and hit the tin. Momentarily, a red corona stained the gloom like a wound. Nancy blinked, and it was just the broad crimson border around the lid. The border framed a picture of a rosy, naked boy with powder blue wings driving a gold chariot pulled by blue dolphins through lilac waves. More blue-winged boys frolicked around the sides of the tin, building pergolas, gathering fruit, weaving garlands of bright pink flowers. One was presenting a pot plant to a man with a yellow towel across his lap. She thought she'd seen that tin before, full of Huntley and Palmer's biscuits, on Aunty Muriel's sideboard. When the light faded, Sadie and Esther silently rocked back on their heels and sat facing one another with the tin between them.

'It is time,' said Sadie.

'It is time,' repeated Esther.

'For the ghosts to show themselves and for us to reveal ourselves to the ghosts . . .' They both looked at Nancy who wrapped her arms around herself, at once suspecting foul play.

'I'm not taking my knickers off!' she said, clutching herself still tighter.

Sadie ignored her. 'We grew out of that sort of thing years ago,' said Esther. 'We're more sophisticated now.' Then, settling herself into an upright, cross legged posture she stroked the fingers of her left hand three times around the picture of the boy and the dolphin, lightly touched each of the blue-winged boys around the sides, opened the tin and laid its contents on the straw table: a creased notebook, a black bic biro, a rabbit's skull, a torch, two unused candles and a paperback book with a broken spine. She picked up the torch and the book, whose brittle pages snapped open at a pre-ordained place. She held the torch beneath her chin, turning her long head into a skull mask and grinned. 'First,' she said, 'we listen to the words of the master.' She flipped the torchlight on to the pages in front of her: 'The most terrifying story ever told. "The Horla", by Guy de Maupassant.' She pronounced Guy in the proper French way and paused, flashing the torch around the barn, streaking their faces with lightning, 'Are you ready?'

'No!' said Sadie loudly. She grabbed the torch, switched it off and lowered her voice to a stage whisper. 'Today, the day of our beloved grandmother's funeral, I have decided we should do something different, something really deep. Are you in?'

'Yes!' whispered Esther, her eyes shining.

'Yes,' said Nancy, her voice shaking.

Sadie rolled sideways and pulled a cloth bundle from the back pocket of her shorts. She shook out the bundle to reveal a large green and purple paisley pattern headscarf made of some silky looking stuff, then she produced the cigarette lighter from her other pocket. 'This,' she said, spreading the scarf out on the straw, 'belonged to Grandma Grace. She was wearing it the day she died . . .'

'How do you know?'

'I just do,' she glared fiercely at Esther. 'And this,' holding up the lighter, 'I nicked from my dad.'

'What are you going to do?' Esther's eyes glittered, her mouth was white with tension.

Sadie looked up wearily. 'Don't rush me,' she said. 'Treat grandma's memory with some respect!' Her eyes were huge and green in the candlelight. 'O.K.,' she said, at last, 'this is going to be our funeral for grandma. A proper one, not all whingeing on about a better place and stuffing bloody bridge rolls and tinned salmon. We're going to summon her up. We will find out what messages she has for us from beyond the grave.' She took the candles from the tin, carefully melted the bases with the cigarette lighter and set them up on the lid. Then she lit the wicks. Nancy shuffled back, hugging her knees; she heard Esther swallow hard. The candlelight rippled and shuddered across their faces, water-washing their features into unrecognisable underground formations. The blue-winged boys, smoke darkened, twisted around the tin like sweet, bad dreams lurking between the roots of trees. Esther gazed fixedly at the candles; Nancy's forehead glistened with sweat. 'Hold hands!' commanded Sadie. 'This is the first phase. You've got to think about her, really think about her. Hard! God, Nancy your hands are so clammy. Close your eyes and try to see her in front of you. Remember what a good and wonderful person she was. In a minute I'm going to raise the sacred headscarf. We each must take a corner and say three really important and special things about our grandmother. To bring her here.'

'Then what'll happen?' asked Esther.

'She'll be here, with us. Esther, if you don't believe in this it won't work.'

'I do believe it, I do!' said Esther, hastily.

'Nancy, do you?'

'Yes.' whispered Nancy.

'Right. Let's just be quiet then.'

They closed their eyes. Nancy screwed hers up as tight as she could and listened to her own breathing. Then she became aware of Sadie pushing a piece of cloth into her left hand and, without anyone giving the word or even a suggestion, they all leaned back together to pull the headscarf taut. Nancy re-adjusted her grip and felt someone else tug her section tighter in response. There was an edgy silence, then Esther began; her voice sounded very odd and not like a twelve year-old girl's at all. It bounced off the scarf like hailstones off a trampoline. Nancy didn't dare look up.

'She had eyes bluer than the sky,' Esther intoned, 'She made flowers grow where nobody else could. She always listened to you.'

Nancy cleared her throat as unobtrusively as possible: 'She made the best coconut cake in the world, she never blamed you for things you didn't do, she didn't tell lies.' She waited, hoping Sadie wasn't going to laugh at her. Sadie didn't laugh. She sat staring at the scarf, she didn't say anything. Esther and Nancy looked up anxiously. For a few seconds nobody breathed. Esther started to say something, very softly. Then Sadie leapt to her feet, snatched the scarf out their hands, so violently Nancy fell backwards, and screamed at the top of her voice: 'She did tell lies! She was an evil old bitch and she told lies all the time. She said I could stay and live with her and granddad for always if I wanted, but they sent me back home. She said she'd watch me in the school play, and she didn't come. She promised I could have her mother-of-pearl box with the earrings in, and that was a lie, I know Aunty Rachel's got it.'

She turned to Nancy, her face bright-red and skewed to one side, 'You've got to get it for me. You've got to get that box off your mother because it's mine, grandma promised it to me.' She grabbed Nancy's shoulders and started shaking her violently, Nancy could hear Esther shouting to her to stop. They were all on their feet now, involved in a weird shuffling dance on the straw, clutching fingers, kicking feet, hair whirling into eyes and mouths, all interlocked limbs and rasping breath. Then, suddenly, Sadie went limp. The three of them dropped back, physically distant from each other, but still pulled into a ragged triangle of eyes and heartbeats. Nancy and Esther breathed hard, they looked at each other, chests rising and falling noisily, wondering if they dared say anything.

Sadie was now quite calm. 'We're better off without her,' she said. Her voice was completely expressionless. She held the scarf up. 'Let's see how this'll burn.'

'Don't,' yelled Esther, lunging at the lid and the still burning candles, but she was too late. Nancy had one last vivid memory of the swift flare of silky material as it hit the flames, Sadie shouting, 'You kicked the tin, you kicked it over, you clumsy cow!' and the rest was a maelstrom of darkness and rasping breath, of feet flapping at the flames, hoarse, tearing laughter, and then Esther was shrieking at them to get out.

Nancy couldn't move, nothing seemed to work, but Esther gripped her arm in a bony stranglehold and dragged her towards the tunnel. There was a roaring sound at their backs and smoke was starting to surge towards them in strange, lurid pulses. Nancy fell face down on the straw, it was rough and hot and alive beneath her. She felt Esther grab her around the chest and yank her to her feet, she couldn't see Sadie, smoke began to fill her mouth and nostrils, she began to choke; Esther was shoving her viciously from behind and the roaring sound completely surrounded them now, only it was no longer an abstract roar, it was crackles and spits, the thunder of straw walls falling and, far above them, the explosive crack of corrugated iron suddenly expanding. Esther pushed her into a gap between some bales, to the right of the tunnel. 'It's the quickest way out. Go, just go! You'll have to jump.' Nancy turned back in panic and saw a field of tiny flames like the red bars of an electric fire rolling towards her across the interior of the stack. Esther launched herself at her, her face was streaked with sweat, her eyes straining out of their sockets, and Nancy was suddenly thrust through a brief passage, so tight the breath left her, and out into the painful bright daylight. She didn't have time to think about the height from which she was jumping, Esther was right behind her and the two of them half fell, half rolled down the wall of bales to the ground.

Nancy drew in lungfulls of air along with the comforting scent of dust and dried excrement. Her blouse was ripped under the arms. Her chest juddered painfully as she gasped for breath. A hank of burnt hair hung limply over Esther's forehead. They looked back at the barn, silent, quivering. From the outside there was no sign of smoke, no fire, no indication that anything was amiss.

'Perhaps it wasn't as bad as we thought,' said Nancy.

'It'll probably just burn itself out,' said Esther. 'They do, when there's a lot of smoke like that.'

They watched the barn anxiously, willing everything to be normal, to be all right. Neither of them could remember afterwards who first noticed that Sadie was missing. Nancy clutched Esther's dress and started shrieking. Esther tore herself free and plunged towards the barn screaming Sadie's name. There was a sudden, huge crash like a house collapsing as the corrugated iron roof shot up into the sky and then fell, in appalling slow motion, back into the barn. The flames, temporarily deprived of oxygen by the crush of falling straw, now leapt free and set fire to the sky. Amid the screaming and the shouts from below as people saw what was happening, the roar of the fire and the cracks and spits of expanding sap inside the horse chestnut tree, Nancy and Esther became aware of Sadie's voice behind them. She had retrieved her skirt from the tree and held it nonchalantly slung over her shoulder with one hand, the other rested on her hip.

'You didn't really think I was still in there, did you?' she said. 'Come on, we'd better get back before they miss us.' Then she turned and started walking coolly away. Nancy and Esther stumbled after her, but Sadie walked faster and faster until she was sprinting ahead of them down the field to meet a party of people fanning out like ashes towards them.

Sadie's father got to her first. He grabbed his daughter's arm, he was breathless and trembling, he looked as if he was going to cry. But Sadie tore away from him and ran to her grandfather. Nancy had never seen granddad so angry. Sadie clung to his jacket, but he pushed her away so hard she fell over and then he started shouting, shouting all sorts of dreadful things about feckless children and a despoiled occasion, about grandma's memory being desecrated, about how she'd have been ashamed of them. Eventually, the other grown-ups managed to calm him down. Sadie got up very slowly from the ground and said, in a terrible voice full of cinders and broken glass,

'I'm glad the stupid barn's on fire. I'm glad she's dead.'

And that was the last thing she said to anybody about the fire in the barn. It took the fire brigade a long time to put it out and the rubble stayed red-hot for nearly a week afterwards. The police cordonned it off and came round to question them all, but still Sadie wouldn't say anything. The farmer didn't, in the end, press charges. Nancy's mother said it was probably because he felt sorry for them, because, after all, it was an accident and Sadie was so poorly afterwards. Aunty Muriel said Sadie's father must have paid him off. Sadie didn't go back to school for a very long time, but nobody would ever explain, in a way that was at all satisfactory, what was wrong with her. When she was well again, Nancy chose one of her best notelets, with a picture of a horse on it, and wrote to say she'd found the mother-of-pearl earring box and that her mum said Sadie could have it. Sadie didn't write back.

DAVID SWANN

A Polder, a Place to Live

Up against the lockers, under his fists. Every dinner-time, same as ever, the crowd of pasty faces.

'Do him do him,' Doyle chants. Welshy's pudgy fists, the titters. And a sour locker smell, whiff of used gym kits and oranges, emptied tupperware.

Drizzle. Always, through the leathering, at the back of it – rain crawling over glass. Then a pause, and some waiting.

Welshy looks at me, says, 'Got you, eh, got you.'

'Do him do him,' chants Doyle.

Welshy's fists again: yellow bits of bones and skin. His hitting comes down – and the girls that watch, they've got pale legs, pleated skirts, green sweaters, stupid ties. Conscientious faraway fists: as if Welshy's proud of his rubbish work, the worst kind of cowboy, a self-deceiver.

'Boring,' says Doyle, squinty-eyed, bog-brush for hair. Had the squishes for the whole term, and still eating the same muck.

'Boring!' goes the chant, the bored chant. Some turn away, girls back in their magazines, the quiet way they turn pages.

Rain, buildings, cooking. The whole world, there, going on.

In close now, Welshy breathing the onion. Last night's meal, his life. Struggling to find the catch, as if he can open me, unroll me.

Fingers into the seams.

'Like that, eh? he says, hands working the bones, searching out soft places.

I know every scratch on this floor, the floor we slide over, our shoes studded with metal plates. I know the place he'll hit me next. My body has the memory for it.

When they hit you, it's only the first hit that hurts. The joke's on him.

His lips pop softly, it's disgusting. Our cheeks touch, and the lockers come open and a vest falls out, a white vest, grey and blue with old sweat. Welshy looks down and stops hitting, there's no more hitting. His eye-corners water. He snuffles, puts a hand in his blazer pocket – as if it's all casual, this savagery, this need, the tears. I watch the wet eye, thinking, Wanker. Thinking, Try that again, go on.

The girls stare at me, the girls ignore me, that quiet page-turning – as if antelopes have seen another antelope felled.

Welsh untwists his tie, the self-consciousness of the hand pushed down into blazer pocket, all the fluff that's probably there. 'You watch it, you,' he says. The fight's gone out of him, he's useless, the feet on him, their pigeon toes.

A bell goes and in comes Mr Cartilage, the white slab of his face. He has never smiled in the thousand years since he was bolted together in a shed. One of those P.E. teachers who pretends to know about Geography. There's a slide-set in his knobbly hand, it's about Dutch sluice gates, how they keep trade moving – and nobody could give a fuck, except maybe it would be interesting if Cartilage shut up.

'I did him,' says Welshy.

'Never,' says Doyle.

'As per usual,' says Welshy. 'Every fucking dinner.'

But Doyle shakes his head, and Welshy knows he's one of those lads who's rubbish at saying fuck, and his head lops.

I'm next to Big Mick, the quiet big lad with the black narrow eyes. 'Doug,' he says, 'why don't you fight him back? Why?'

I slide back into the seat, this melted seat, they set a bunsen burner on it. And Big Mick's watching me, narrow eyes, as if somewhere underneath there's the real Big Mick. 'Don't know,' I tell him, but the words hardly come out, it's like a croak.

This is the Big Mick: taught himself kung-fu but never mentions it; got off with someone's wife in a chip shop but won't discuss it; bought a can of McEwan's lager on the school trip to Edinburgh and took it somewhere quiet, away from everyone. Big lad, into the music that you're into because your older cousin says it's great – but you're not into it really, and Big Mick is.

How must it sound to him, this throat croak, these words that barely come out?

Big Mick refuses to say any more about it.

Cartilage drones. He has so much face that there is barely room for eyes, they are tiny currants on a batter cake.

The opening of the sluice.

An equalisation of water levels.

Lights go off, the same old slide-set. In the dark, Welshy is bawking, splatters that glitter in the dark on his brown skin, tears as fat as you'd expect.

I nudge Big Mick to look, but he stares at the slides, long mop of hair down nearly to his narrow eyes. The way those eyes can fix you, and that's enough. His pale face: he probably stays in probably shagging probably wanking probably whatever it is that Big Mick does when he stays in. He does whatever he likes – as if he knows this is a waste of time, not even important enough to ignore.

But sometimes I look at the straight line of Big Mick's shoulders and he's clamping down, like I do when Welshy's at me. Ready for it.

One who has nothing to lose is on the other side of me: Millett, a stick of a kid, who wears black jeans to school. The teachers never even look at him. Skinny tie, rolled-up sleeves, the bones on him. 'Did you see it? It was ace, did you see it?' His grey lips lack any spit.

The sluice gates are totally regulated, they are reliable in all weathers.

'That space ship they've got,' says Millett. It's some telly programme he's on about, one that kids like him watch. I know. I watch it.

'The mother ship,' says Millett, and he rolls and rolls at his sleeves. He has sharp elbows, and a thin nose. His hair will all fall out in one day when he's 23-years old, wooooosh, gone. 'Warp thrust!' he hisses. 'That ship! With the warp thrust!'

There is nowhere you can look, not at Millett, not at Big Mick, not at Welshy, definitely not at Cartilage, his eyeless visage. He makes you think of tendon.

Doyle drops his guts. SBD: Silent But Deadly. 'Good arse,' he says, satisfied with his work. Everyone moves their chairs, holds their noses – everyone except Welshy, who's as far off as I am when he beats me. It's almost as if we aren't mates, but we are. We were mates before we even came to this school, when it didn't matter that he had pigeon-toes and two arses, the weird potatoey shape on him.

I remember the first time I say him, at the old school. We were 9-year olds, he was new. He had brown eyes that watched – kind and scared, both at once.

'I was the top scorer in my real school,' said Welshy. He stood in the dip of the yard, the place where all the water runs to. 'I got 20 goals,' he said.

'Which school?'

'In another town,' he said. He flapped his hand towards the hills. A big blowy place, white grass and no trees. 'My dad,' he said, 'he came to watch every match.'

I didn't tell him that I never scored. I was a right-back, which is virtually a goal-keeper, you never go near the other nets.

'We were top of the league,' he said.

'Smart.'

He said, 'What's your name?'

'Doug Roper.'

'How many goals have you scored?'

'Eighteen.'

The wind blew. I looked down at the bumpy tarmac. His feet pointed inwards.

'That's two less then me,' he said.

The lights come on. Suddenly everyone in the classroom is writing.

Millett won't let me be free. 'That ship, the mother ship – it can fly to The Edge of the Known Universe,' he whispers. 'It's got a turbo-boost.'

And: 'Permanent water supply on the Planet of Mars.'

'Millett,' I beg, 'what are they writing?'

And: 'Sealed docking manoeuvre.'

'With their pencils. What are they writing?'

This is what the pencils sound like: like a forest, closing – trees folding in after you've gone through them, like they're whispering, like pencils, like Millett.

If I don't stop him, we will be hammered. 'Millett,' I tell him, 'shut up!'

'Roper!' Cartilage says. 'Have you something to say, Roper?'

'Sir, no, sir.'

The class laughs. I try to growl but it's too dark and his skeleton hand is at the corner of his mouth, skinny lips barely moving, going, 'Reverse thrust system.'

'Sir, Doug Roper is still talking, sir,' says Doyle.

Cartilage stands up, no warning. The thick body that needs no warning. He looks down over the class as if it's the massive sea. 'Everyone. Quiet,' he says. The thumb of his face comes to rest on Doyle. The only thing I can find to like about Cartilage: he hates Doyle, has no time for him. 'Read your answer, Doyle.'

Doyle looks at his scribble, helpless. Cartilage passes over. 'Sandra,' he commands, 'tell this cretin what a polder is.'

Sandra is one of the featureless waves. 'Polders are reclaimed land in Holland,' she reads. 'The sea is pumped out to create land for people to live on.'

Cartilage says, 'See me later, Doyle.' He has a colourless voice, like dough. There isn't any reason in him. He won't bleat to us like the ones who beg for mercy.

'And they hurtled into another dimension,' says Millett from behind his hand.

The lights go out again. Click. Another slide.

We move on through the afternoon, hearing the beating of rain behind the dark blinds.

There is a scenic quality to many of the villages that line the shores of the former Zuider Zee.

All the time, Welshy looks down, looks down, this soft stare at the desk, the desk he defaced last week – but only underneath, which is typical of him. 'Look,' he told us, 'look – I've done this desk!' He had to turn it over, and books fell off. Where the teachers don't look, he'd scratched twat and bollocks, written BFC, though that's not his team. No team, two arses. That's just about typical. And it's all because of his feet and his dad. If it weren't for that, he'd not kick my head in every dinner-time and I wouldn't be bothered about his lumpy two-arse shape, and we'd be proper best mates, not best mates that hate each other.

I saw what they did to Millett. It was after school on the green by the bus stops. He looked back, stumbled, and then he was lost. They fell on him, a big gang.

When he got up out of the wet grass, clay smeared over him, stringy bits and cuts, he just carried on walking, he didn't look back. It impressed me.

They booted the freckles off him.

Doyle was there, he must rent time on an American spy satellite. 'Ha! Planet of Mars!' he grinned. 'Got it in the chops!' and Millett was pushed and shoved by Doyle because he had already been beaten to the ground by other boys, strangers.

These strangers, they were at another school. They had stupid blazers on. Millett didn't know them.

Some kids know their targets before they see them. They lock on, like spaceships. They go through walls. Before you know it, they're coming down on you, out of the sky. Millett stumbled, and that cost him. It must have hurt; he hasn't got the skin, no padding.

The places that Millett walked into, the people he got battered by: they were strange to him. He was all at sea.

'Why do you never fight back?' Big Mick had asked me.

You just can't explain it.

On the first day I met Welshy, we played penalties. He was quite good, but he tripped over his feet. Then he missed a sitter that I'd have put away.

'The wind,' he said.

'What wind?'

'It bent my shot. At my other school, it's not windy. I got 20 goals.'

'You said.'

'Don't you believe me? I'm a natural goal-scorer. If you're good at sport, it makes you popular.' He looked at his watch. It was golden, and had silent ticks. 'This watch,' he said, 'it cost a packet.'

'Does it tell the right time?'

'Tell the right time, 'course it tells the right time!' He gave me a look, like he felt sorry for me, which was weird because I thought the same about him.

'We can play for a bit longer, if you like,' I offered.

'Can't. My mates are waiting for me. We've synchronised our digital watches.'

'I didn't know what that meant. 'Tomorrow?'

'Might do,' said Welshy. He kicked the ball to me. 'I've got a good all-round game, my dad told me. He comes to watch every game. Boomf!' Welshy pretended to kick. 'In the old onion bag, that's what my dad calls it. A saying he's got.'

'Is he a footballer, too, your dad?'

'He used to be,' said Welshy, and ran to meet his mates with the watches.

Who else has been terrorised?

Three teachers on the sick, including the maths bloke with the green eyes and small hands, Creeley. It was a stroke. Someone saw the weak thing in him, a tiny crack, and we prised at it for weeks.

Weeks and weeks.

He put a lot of brylcream in his hair, you could imagine him staring into the mirror in the mornings, before he came to school.

'Hello, children,' he said, at first. Then he stopped staying it. Then he tried to turn back the tide.

'There will be changes,' he said.

'A new regime,' he said.

Rumours came down to us that the fifth formers had backed him into a curtain and pummelled him. It emboldened us.

Welshy said that Creeley was a pervert. Creeley was a county badminton champion. He knew all the positions on the court. The only harm in him was his weakness. It terrified us.

He taught us about sub-sets, circles that cut through each other.

They tied an elastic band to a divider. Then they flicked a rubber at Creeley. We bust our guts laughing. It went right past his nose.

'How could you miss?' said Doyle, and he had a rolled-up cone over his nose.

Welshy grabbed the cone and blew through it. 'PERP!' he shouted. 'PERPP!'

'Welshy,' said Creeley.

'Sir, do you like my hooter, sit? It's a hooter.'

This was all because Creeley had a big nose.

'Give that to me,' said Creeley. And he grabbed for the cone. 'Give it to me, give it to me.'

Welshy held on.

Only Doyle laughed. The rest of us were quiet, watching – even Millett, who studied his pale blue arms, who didn't look, while Welshy and the teacher fought over the cone, tugging, tugging. As if it really was the teacher's nose.

Rain swarmed over the windows.

Films with fights in them are lies. The fists in films, you'd think a tree had fallen over. This is a real fight: shhhh shhhh, breath noises and soft things, concentration on faces, a rustling of polyester blazers, sleeves over waxy desk tops.

Creeley's silver cufflink catching and clicking on the edges.

Then the nose came away in Creeley's hand and there was a moment when he didn't know what to do with it, his own nose, and nobody else did either.

He used to smile, but now he never did.

'Unfair?' he shouted, more shocking to us than if he had sworn.

He raised the nose to strike Welshy, but Welshy, who was crying, didn't flinch, he stared. He had made himself scared so he could be brave, and it was nearly the end for Mr Creeley, he wouldn't be telling us much more about circles that cut through each other, that divided sets, which we always pronounced as 'sex'.

Sir, can we talk about sex again today, sir?

Sir, sex, sir!

Sir, what is it about sex that fascinates you, sir?

So the door came open while he was ready to smash to pieces – using a version of his own nose – the tearful head of a second-former. And he was absolutely luckless, it was the head mistress.

'Mr Creeley?' she said.

He looked back at her. She had a tight little nose that no air could get up, glasses that pinched it. Her tiny nose, his hooter. It was an insult.

Miss Dray's glasses were solid black, they flared out to gigantic horns. 'Can I talk to you, Mr Creeley?' she said. Normally she shouted. This was serious, it was the same level tone she used to tell us about the dismantling of our empire, the gunboat Panther they sent to Agadir. Our empire was not like other empires.

'Yes, Miss Dray,' he said in a low, beaten voice.

He was a small harmless guy with a thin neck. He was going to have a stroke.

He put his hair back, fussed it to a quiff, and I smelled the brylcream. It made me sad, I hated him for that.

They were gone. Nobody spoke, and then everybody did. The girls put hands over their mouths and gasped. Welshy's eyes gleamed. Sandra, the tall one with the thick legs and ruddy face, nudged her friend Lynn, a girl I never noticed much. Lynn stared at the rainy glass and said, 'Amazing!' in a dreamy voice, as if it was wonderful, but not good to look at.

Millett said, 'That was like this programme I saw . . .'

Sparrowy twitters, a roar of unbroken voices.

'It was in outer space,' said Millett, nudging me with the point of his elbow.

'Yes,' I said. He had big hooded watchful eyes that never blinked. He was looking right at me, orange-coloured boy with skeleton hands.

I watched Lynn, the dreamy one. I knew she was pretending to listen to Sandra, but loved all this and couldn't bear it, that she watched the rain because the rain's the usual old stuff, it makes you safe.

Only one person kept quiet: Big Mick, as mysterious as coal. His eyes had narrowed to slits, shoulders a solid line.

Gossip moved like water.

It was in the school hall.

They got him against some curtains . . .

They punched the shite out of him!

A scowl bit a hole in Doyle's face. He was little, creeping, sinister. 'Shhhh!' he said, 'shhhh! Everyone. To listen. To hear.'

Then Miss Dray came back. She was a travelling cloud of vengeance, as mighty as an empire. Her silence was louder than our noise. She didn't speak, she looked out from the enormous horns, taking in each face. Snipping, gathering.

Then she was gone again, and, as the door swished shut, I saw Mr Creeley, standing alone in the corridor. He was pretending to hum, like a bus might be coming. His eyes hadn't got anything to do with music, they were hurt eyes, like Welshy's.

Even Doyle shut up.

From the corridor came low tones, and I knew – by the dull red floor and the rain on the glass and the dented lockers – that our maths teacher, who had a kind voice, who wore clean shirts and had small careful hands and who knew exactly where to stand on the badminton court, that this harmless little man, who had somehow made us hate him, even though there was nothing wrong with him, would be going away for a long time.

And when he returned, just for one week, in many months' time, he would blink at the wrong moment and we would finish the job, and a stroke would take him.

It would be Miss Dray who came back to us, and she would be terrifying.

The first time Welshy beat me up in front of everyone at dinner-time, it was a mistake. I forgave him. 'Don't worry,' I said as we walked home.

'You were asking for it, though,' he said, and his eyes were wet, they were always wet, I was sick of how soft he was.

'You got me against the lockers,' I said.

'You shouldn't have made me do it.'

'I didn't mean to.'

'The way you were looking at me,' he said.

'What way?'

Welshy didn't answer. He swung his bag over his shoulder. It was full of books.

'Is that homework?' I said.

Welshy said, 'Only puffs do homework.'

'Oh, only I thought it was homework.'

'Are you saying I'm a puff?'

Cars gleamed with rain. The sun had come out, there was a crack of blue sky. You can't trust it.

When we got to my house, Welshy said, 'I'll see you tomorrow.'

He walked away, his stupid feet, his arses. The bag bulged. A watery shadow went with him, and faded.

Way down at the other end of the street, he wasn't a big fat cushion of a boy any more, he was small and on his own, and it didn't matter how often he battered me, it wouldn't bring back his dad.

For the rest of our lives, we will be in this darkened room, behind the blinds, watching slides of dykes and canals taken in drizzly conditions in northern Europe.

Eventually, Cartilage will reach the section on Rotterdam and become almost emotional. He will quote facts to us about tonnages and shipments. He will repeatedly use the phrase, *Europoort, a vast dock*. 'From this vast dock, cargo is distributed' – and just for a few seconds the cold lard of his voice will be slightly softer – 'to faraway destinations such as Vancouver and Rio de Janeiro.' And it might even occur to you that Cartilage lives in a house and has a wife and feeds his cat.

'Cartilage is obsessed with Europoort,' says Doyle. He kicks the pavement, spits. 'Bloody nutter. See the way he went on at me?'

Welshy and me don't say anything. It's battering it down. The walk always seems longer when Doyle comes with us.

'I reckon he's got shares in Europoort,' he says.

We keep our heads down. Cars and lorries chuck surf at our ankles.

'Stocks and shares, and that,' says Doyle.

The rain has got us beaten, there aren't any dry places. Welshy says, 'You don't even know what they are.'

Doyle is wide in the eye. 'I bloody do!' he rages. 'My dad's got investments. I know what stocks and shares are.'

Welshy makes a sound with his lips. Doyle pushes Welshy into the stained wall. Welshy looks down, there's spit and drizzle on

Doyle's mouth. He gets in close at Welshy's ear, hisses, 'What would you know? You haven't even got a dad!'

Welshy looks back at him from the side of his eye.

Tomorrow, at dinner-time, when it's raining and the girls are quietly turning pages, Welshy will come to my desk and say, 'You're one of them lads that never stands up for their mates.'

I won't speak, and Big Mick will turn away. Then Doyle will be by Welshy, going: 'Do him do him' and Welshy will say, 'Starting? Are you starting?' and I'll turn to the side, first punch to the kidney, the one that hurts.

'This is what you get if you don't stand up for your mates,' Welshy will say.

'Show him, Welshy.' I will pull him to me, near, inside his onion breath, and his fist won't be able to go back far enough. This close, miles from punches, I'll find the place that no-one else knows about, that even Millett's mother ship can't reach.

'You're starting, I'm finishing,' Welshy will say, words off the telly. Another punch. 'Do you like hospital food? Want to pick your teeth up with a broken arm?'

I'll see Sandra, excited, breathless, the one that knows about polders. The fat fists will come in and she'll push Lynn, and Lynn will nod and look through me to the window, where the rain clings.

'Fight-FIGHT! Fight-FIGHT!'

Doyle will push Welshy to beat me and Welshy will need to do it because I saw Doyle beat him.

It won't be any use, I'll keep my eyes on the scratched floor, pretend nobody's watching. But I will look at Millett and he'll be whistling, as if another bus is late, and my beating will remind him of what's waiting for him, the bullies he does not know, bullies with no gentleness in them, who have not even had their dads die.

It's late now, and cold, I lie in bed. Sometimes I wet it. I'll wake up when it's still dark, and find the sheets warm. What you must do then is find a dry place and forget it. But the worst thing is, later, when the warmth has gone and the coldness of the piss wakes you, and it's still dark.

I turn again, to a dry place. No-one has seen any of this. I'm safe.

There's a big pump, working and working. A crowd of Netherlanders till it. The pump goes on with it, the clackety-clack of the drainage.

Far off, a big ship sails over the ocean. Everyone waves. The ship's hooter is a blessing.

I smile at the Netherlander working beside me, Big Mick. The pump goes clackety-clack in its drainage.

Soon the sea-bed will be a polder, and the polder will be a place to live.

BENJAMIN PORTUS

Welcome to Cairo

You can smell Islamic Cairo as you come down off the flyover. It rises through the reek of pollution: a soapy perfume so thick and sweet on the hot, dusty air, that you can feel it pouring like syrup through your taxi window. As you open the door the heavy atmosphere floods in, pushes sanity out, and throws you into the jaws of a bright new world, which promptly swallows you whole in its haste. I stood in the belly of Egyptian life and I stared.

'Awesome,' said Joe. He flapped his arms at the scene and snorted with excitement. 'Look at this place.'

There was colour everywhere. Banners hung between shop roofs against a blue-sky backdrop. Technicolour galabiyyas swayed on their lines, gold braid on jet-black, crimson with blue, green with white, as far as I could see. Lower down and shirts, ties, ladies' scarves, all lay in vast piles. Tables strained under the weight of the rich harvest: straddled yet more of the lush crop of clothes. We were approached within seconds.

'Welcome to Cairo my friends. You English? I love English man. You know Manchester United? Yeah man, Michael Owen. How long you been here? You like Papyrus my friends? Genuine papyrus, look my friends. Only ten Egyptian pounds. Just look man . . . no charge for looking, hey. Come back. You don't have to buy. I love English. For English, five pounds . . .'

We swept into the street.

'Welcome in Cairo.'

'Welcome my friends.'

'Everything free.'

'Welcome my friends.'

'Hey. Hey! You like? Look here . . .'

'You want spices? You want?'

'Welcome.'

'Hello.'

'Hello.'

'Very good price my friends.'

'Welcome my friends, welcome in Cairo.'

'Hello.'

'Baksheesh baksheesh.'

I tried to speak to all of them; smiled at every one. I loved their politeness and hated our tightness. I bought a hat and haggled the shopkeeper out of a few pounds. To me it was nothing: to him perhaps a meal, or a pair of shoes. I bought some cheap pens and handed them out to the children who followed in ever increasing numbers. I swapped addresses with a boy who clutched to his chest a carrier bag filled with the letters sent to him from other tourists he had successfully accosted. By the end of the street I was elated and tired, and Joe had lost his patience.

'I need to sit down.'

'Me too. Let's get some food.'

We found a kushari joint and collapsed. We argued with the proprietor about the price, and eventually paid the going rate when we threatened to find somewhere else to eat. We gulped tepid water from a plastic bottle and sighed. I smiled.

'It's just amazing.'

'It's overwhelming.' Joe shook his head. 'It's over-bloody-whelming.'

We ate quickly and talked between mouthfuls about what we would do next. It was midday. We decided to brave the bazaars once more and do some of our holiday shopping together.

'Let's do spices first,' said Joe.

'OK.' I said. 'Let's do it.'

We trekked past stinking fishmongers and looked open-mouthed at the butchers. They left tails on the skinned carcasses – the only way you could tell what species you were having for dinner. When we got to the spice stalls I braced myself.

'Hello, you English?'

'Bloody hell,' muttered Joe.

'Relax,' I said, 'Deep breaths.' I turned towards the voice.

'Hi there. Yes, we're English.' I smiled. I wanted to be polite. I was the visitor after all.

'Don't worry guys,' said the Egyptian. 'I'm not from any shop or anything. Don't worry.'

'Like hell,' whispered Joe.

'Are you guys new in Cairo?'

'No.' I smiled some more. 'We've been here a couple of months now. Travelling round. We went up to Siwa, then down to Aswan, up to Luxor, then here.' I drew a map in the air with my finger. It was a lie of course, but it prevented the more crude con-artists from bothering. We had been in Egypt for just two days.

'You like?'

'Excellent. Yeah, really beautiful. I love these markets. They're so exciting.' I waved about me. Joe was looking at nothing, trying desperately not to be leapt on by another over enthusiastic salesman, trying desperately not to listen to the stranger who was now beside us. I didn't like Joe's narrow way of thinking. Tiredness was no excuse for his rudeness. I took the conversation further, partly out of genuine interest, partly to irritate my companion.

'You students yeah?'

'Yes. We're at different universities though. I'm at Bristol, he's at London.'

'Ah, London. I have a friend in London.'

'Really? Have you been to England?'

'No. I love England, but I've not been there. I hear a lot about England.'

'England is nice. It's very different to here. I love Egypt though. The people have been very friendly.'

'You look worried my friend. You English always look worried. Smile, hey? You don't have to worry about me. I am not after your money my friend. A lot of people, they think all Egyptian after money and think of nothing else. I just like to practise my English. I am rich. Look.' He took out his wallet and showed me how rich he was.

'Oh, no. No. I believe you. Honestly. We have to be careful though, you must understand.' Silence. 'You live here in Cairo?'

'Yes. I study here now.'

'Oh right. What do you study?'

'I study law. Here in Cairo I study law.'

'Joe studies law at London, don't you Joe.'

'You study law as well Joe?'

Joe turned around reluctantly. 'Yeah,' he said. 'I've got two years to go until I finish studying.'

'Me also. I also have two years to go 'til I finish studying.'

'What will you do when you finish?'

'I have uncle in Australia. I will go and work with my rich uncle in Australia when I finish. I want to practise my English before I go. I want to practise English with you, that's all my friends – you understand now? Would you like me to show you around the bazaars?'

Joe didn't want to go around the bazaars. I told him not to be such a bigot. In the end it was a compromise: we'd go with the man but only for ten minutes, and we'd leave at once if things got at all dodgy. The Egyptian looked in dismay at our hushed argument over this matter.

'I'm not after your money my friend. Please, don't think all Egyptian like that. It hurts me. I just want to practise English, you know?'

'I'm sorry. We're coming. It's very kind of you to take us around. You're very kind.'

'We just have to be careful,' said Joe. 'You understand? We have met some people and they say they are our friends and they just want us to buy duty free alcohol for them, or go to their papyrus museum.'

'I not like that. I'm rich. I'm not after your money. Look.'

'OK. We'll come with you. Thank you. We'll go a little way.'

The back streets were narrower. Empty of westerners. We stopped to watch a woman who sat, dressed in black, cross-legged on the dirt. She took gasping pigeons one by one from their cramped cages and fed them, squirting white liquid from her mouth into the upturned beaks. The pigeons sat bemused wherever they were plonked down, making no attempt to fly away. She spat any remaining liquid into the street, then refilled her mouth from a canister beside her and repeated the process.

'This is the factory. You know? They make the . . . the, er, precious stones?'

'Alabaster?'

'Yes. They make the al-lab-as-tur, is that right? They make it into all these beautiful things. See?'

There was a small dark room, open to the street. The men inside turned lathes. They hobbled to and fro on crippled limbs. The tables and floors were covered in stone and wood chippings. The shelves were stacked to breaking point with the same chess sets and jars and photo frames seen everywhere around the city.

'Hello English,' said one of the older workers.

'Hello.' I smiled. Our guide talked for several minutes to the men in the factory. They laughed loudly at what he said and looked at us with shiny wet eyes.

'He's blatantly going to try and rip us off in a minute,' said Joe.

'I don't think so. You can't just judge him like that. He could be just a genuine nice guy.'

'Why would he want to show us around? Hasn't he got anything better to do?'

'Maybe he's just being friendly. Learning English like he said. Why shouldn't we trust him?'

'He didn't even know the word for alabaster. I mean, isn't alabaster an Egyptian word? It sounds Egyptian to me. All Egyptians know what alabaster is don't they? Just look at him. He knows all these people. He talks to all of them. He probably does this all the time.'

'He's studying law.'

'Whatever.'

The man finished his conversation and the workers all waved and smiled at us, eyes twinkling out from the gloom. We walked beside him as he told us about the different things we saw. He took us to the outside of a mosque, which was special, he said, because only widows or unmarried women were allowed to use it. We looked through the bars and saw women walking slowly past, some wearing the wrinkles of suffering, others the smoothness of virginity.

'See. He's telling the truth. He's just a nice guy.'

'We should go soon. Ten minutes you agreed.'

He took us down some more alleyways and again said that we shouldn't worry, that he was rich and didn't want to rip us off. We said we had things to do, and he asked what those things were, so I told him that we wanted to buy some spices. Joe dug me hard in the ribs. The man led us to a different spice stall from the one where we had met him and talked to the keeper. Joe glared at me.

'You can buy good spice here. No obligation, you understand. I get you good price too – real Egyptian price, not tourist price. You are my friends OK?'

I sat down first. Joe – reluctant and moaning – sat down beside me. The keeper came over and handed us small samples of the different spices available, each one balanced on a square of white paper. We passed them between us and sniffed and nodded at the different smells. Joe noticed that the pieces of paper were taken from some scientific journal or other. He looked cheerful for almost the first time since we'd left the taxi.

'Look,' he said. 'It's in English as well.' He read from one of the sheets. 'A total of twenty-one male Sprague-Dawley rats were used in this study. Rats were anaesthetised with Equithesin . . . er,' he paused, 'bla bla bla, before exposure of the inferior alveolar nerve. A small skin incision overlying the masseter muscle and blunt dissection of the underlying tissue exposed the mandible. A small bur hole in the mandible was made with a high-speed dental drill to expose the inferior alveolar nerve in the mandibular canal and a pair of number fifteen jeweller's forceps were used to crush the inferior alveolar nerve.' He stopped. 'That's all there is on this piece. What about yours?'

I was trying to smell some curry powder and Joe went to grab the square of paper off me. 'Joe!' I snatched it back and the powder went flying. 'You prick! Now look what you've done.' The empty sheet was in my hand and orange powder was scattered across my lap.

'Sorry,' he said. 'I was only trying to look at the writing. You didn't have to get all stroppy.'

'I wasn't getting stroppy. I was trying to smell the spices. That is what we're here for isn't it? I don't want to listen to you banging on about some poor rat having its nerves crushed or whatever crap that was, do I?'

'You've thrown it away?' said the keeper in dismay. 'Why you throw it away hey?' He turned to our guide and spoke in Egyptian.

'You can pay?' said our guide. He pointed at my lap.

'Yes. Of course,' I said. 'I'm really sorry. We didn't mean to waste the curry powder. I'll pay.' I looked at Joe and frowned. 'God only knows why, but I'll pay,' I whispered.

I bought some other spices and paid for the spilt curry powder. Despite looking guilty Joe refused to spend anything on principle. When we had left the shop, he spoke to our Egyptian friend before I could say anything.

'We have to go now,' he said. 'You've been very kind. Thank you for showing us all these things, but we're going.'

Our guide looked hurt.

'You do not trust me my friends? I do not understand. You think all Egyptian like hassling?'

'No. You've been very kind. Thank you. I hope that your law study goes well, but we have to go.'

'Where you go now?'

'We are going. We are going back to our hotel.'

'Which hotel?'

'Good bye.'

Joe walked off. I looked at the Egyptian.

'Thank you. You've been very kind. My friend is just tired. Sorry. I must go or I'll lose him. Sorry we spilt the curry powder. Thank you.'

We stood beside the main road and argued, our voices rising above the roar of traffic. We decided it would be best to split up. Sod off was how Joe put it: there was no way he was being dragged around by a blatant con-artist while his stupid friend nodded and smiled like an idiot. We agreed to meet up at the hotel at five.

'How was your afternoon?' I said when I got in. I collapsed on a plastic chair in the kitchen and ran my fingers through my hair. I was weary.

'It was good.' Joe was sipping a coke. He stood up and got me one from the fridge. He sat back down and looked sheepish. 'Sorry,' he said.

'What for?'

'For not believing you. For not trusting that man. It was bad of me.'

'Bloody sensible, that's all.'

'It was terrible. I shouldn't have judged him like I did. I've learnt a lot this afternoon.'

'Oh?'

'I met a cart driver. I thought sod it, I'm not walking, my feet are knackered. Anyway, he gave me a ride. He didn't want any money. He took me back to his house. It's been an amazing afternoon. He was the nicest person . . . and his family too. They were so nice you wouldn't believe it.'

'Tell me all about it,' I said. I rested my head in my hands. It hurt.

'Right. First of all I said that I wanted to go to the end of the street. Really I did it because, like I said, I was tired and getting hassled. I started chatting. Just the normal stuff. It turned out that he had four kids and a wife who was ill and his horse hadn't been fed.

'Well you know me. I was sat there thinking here we go, he's going to do the hard sell on me and ask for ten quid or something. Well, I said to him that I would love to go and see his family – really I didn't believe him and I wanted to see how genuine he was.

'"We'll go along now if you like," he said. I agreed, thinking he would duck out and ask for money at the last minute. Anyway, he took me for miles and miles. I was thinking oh bugger, I've done it now: this is either going to end in me being mugged or asked for tons of cash and abandoned in the middle of nowhere. We went into this really dodgy alleyway that he said he lived in and I started looking around and shitting myself.

'"This is it," he said and pointed to this tall shabby building. It looked like the kind of place that lone travellers get murdered in. My heart was pounding. I was cursing myself for being so stupid. He led me down a side passage, then up some stairs, and then he introduced me to his family.

'It was awesome. They were so nice. Here, look.' He fished in his bag for something. It was a small picture on a scrap of paper. 'Their little kid gave it to me. It's supposed to be me. Cute hey? They gave me cups of tea and we talked for ages. I think that there were other people in the house, his sister and that, but they didn't come out. They were too shy.

'I got their address.' He put another scrap of paper on the table. 'I'm going to write back. They were so nice. So I'm sorry I was worried this morning about that bloke, and I think that you were probably right about him.'

I shrugged and didn't know what to say. I didn't know whether to tell Joe about my afternoon or not. I decided that telling him would spoil the happy ending.

'I'm really pleased that you met such nice people,' I said. 'I don't think you were wrong to be careful though. Let's call it quits shall we?' We agreed on quits.

'I've got to go to the toilet,' I said.

'OK.'

I stood up, and Joe noticed the stains on my trousers.

'Horse shit. I fell over. Stupid.'

He laughed for ages. I locked myself in the toilet and cried.

Joe crossed the footbridge and I was on my own. I didn't really know what to do, but I felt a strong desire to prove my friend wrong.

We had known each other for ten years. Joe had supported me when my brother had died, and I had supported him throughout numerous girlfriend problems. We hadn't really seen each other since joining university: brief glances during work-packed holidays; brief telephone calls to confirm our living status. We'd decided to travel to get to know each other again. I now wanted to prove to Joe that I'd become more mature, worldly and generally open-minded than him. I retraced my footsteps towards the spice stall we had just left.

'Ah, my friend you are back.' I heard the familiar voice.

'I left Joe behind.' I laughed. 'He didn't want to trust you. I'm sorry. Some people can be stupid when they're in a strange place.

'My friend don't worry. Would you like some tea? We can make you some nice tea now.'

'That would be brilliant.' I was feeling smug already. I sat where I had been just minutes before and waited while the Egyptian went and made some tea. When he brought it to me it was very hot and sweet. It was served in a tall glass, and a thick layer of green leaves had settled in the bottom.

'Mint,' he said when I looked at the leaves. 'Very good mint tea. You like?'

I took a sip and burnt my lip. I nodded. I liked very much. I blew on the surface.

'Hot?'

'Very hot. Very nice though. Thank you. You're kind.'

'No problem my friend. You want me to show you more of bazaars when you finished?'

'Please. I'd like that very much.'

'No problem my friend.'

I carried on drinking, watching my guide having a dynamic and humorous conversation with the owner of the spice shop. They must have talked about me at one point – they looked around at my cautious sipping and laughed. I smiled. When I had finished I thanked the owner and fell into conversation with my guide as we walked.

'Do your family live in Cairo as well?'

'Oh no. My family in Aswan. I come here to study. My brother works here in Cairo so I stay with him.'

'What does your brother do?'

He tried to explain. 'He . . . you know. Fixes big . . .' he made grabbing motions with his hands, then lifted them upwards.

'Cranes? For lifting things.'

'Yes. He fixes them. How do you say? Ker-rane?'

'Crane.'

'Yes. He fixes them. Here in Cairo.' We walked in silence for a while. My guide was less talkative now and I struggled to think of questions.

'Have you been in the army yet?'

'No. Not yet. I join for one year when I finish my study. My brother – he was in the army for three years. He didn't finish education, see? But I will finish my education here in Cairo, so for me only one year.'

We walked down a very narrow alleyway. The street was rougher. Dirty water filled potholes that I skirted around carefully. Bundles of sugar cane lay on each side, emaciated donkeys picking wearily through them, looking for traces of nutrition. I stepped over a pile of steaming dung. The air was dusty, filled with smells of animal shit and rotting fish. It was noisy with people: the sounds of moaning and coughing, the growl of phlegm being sucked back and spat out. A lone child played with a mangy dog until his mother shouted at him: then he kicked it instead and it ran off whining. My guide stopped.

'This is my house,' he said.

'You live here?' I couldn't contain my surprise. I saw that he noticed it.

'You don't like my house?'

'Oh. No. Not at all. I mean, I love it. It's great. Real Egyptian house. I love it. It's just . . . very different to England.'

'In England you have clean houses?'

'Well . . .'

'We don't need clean house here. We have Allah my friend. Egyptian, they work hard my friend. All day we work hard. But we don't need clean house my friend.'

'Really. It's lovely. I'm sorry I looked surprised. It's just . . . different, like I said. It's lovely. Your brother lives here as well?'

'Yes. He's probably up there right now. You want to meet him? To see inside? It's nice inside, you will like. You want tea. I have tea for you my friend.'

'I shouldn't be long.'

'You have to return? You are worried again my friend. I can see.'

'No. Not worried.' I gulped. I was determined to prove Joe wrong. I smiled. 'I would love to see inside. You're very kind.'

It was dark in the stair well. It stank of piss. There was no banister and I tripped once and put my hand down on some filthy slime. I wiped it on my trousers and carried on walking.

His room was on the third floor, and we were greeted with a

gruff, aggressive voice from somewhere unseen. My guide replied with a shout, and a rapid exchange between the two men followed.

The main room was tiny. There was a sofa and pictures on the walls. There was a heavy wooden candlestick, empty of any candle, on a rickety old table. There was an old black and white television, which flicked silent shadows onto the walls. I watched the programme. A woman was standing in court being cross-examined, and there appeared to be a lot of shouting, the mute faces screwed up, furious gesticulations. The woman started crying. The snowy interference of the screen made my eyes ache so I gave up watching it.

'Wait here,' said my Egyptian friend.

'Thank you. No problem.'

I sat on the sofa. There was no window. The floor was bare and there was no bulb on the cord that ran from a hole in the cracked white ceiling. Scant lighting came from the corridor my guide had disappeared into. I bit my nails, then leant back on the sofa, trying to relax.

There were stains on the wall behind the sofa. I sat back up and turned around to look closer, and my heart began to pound. They were brown stains: blood, no mistake – a short streak running at head height behind the sofa, little spots bursting out from it. I looked at my hand, at the fingernails I had so recently chewed. More blood . . . from the stairs where I had tripped. It was drying, going crusty. There was a big brown hand-shaped stain on my trousers. The soles of my shoes were still wet . . . still red. There were footprints on the floorboards, which blended in with the wood so that they were almost unnoticeable.

Fuck.

I stood up and walked in a circle.

Stupid stupid fucking idiot.

I went to the door. I turned, looked down the corridor towards the light. The voices carried on, arguing now, getting more and more rapid.

Arguing about me? Of course. Arguing about whether or not to do me in. Trying to decide if I'm worth it. Trying to decide if I've told my English friend where I am. Trying to decide if I've got much money on me. What a stupid idiot I am!

I sat back down and tried to think. I looked at the stains and my panic rose.

They could be innocent. There could have been an accident . . . anything could have happened.

I heard movement coming towards the room and in that same instant my survival instinct took over. I grabbed the wooden candlestick and waited behind the wall. I saw the shadow of a man approaching: getting longer and longer. Then I smashed the candlestick into the face of the approaching person as hard as I could.

And I ran.

This, I guess, is the postscript. Or whatever you want to call it.

I'm sitting on my bed and my arms ache from propping myself up to write. Joe is asleep beside me. He's snoring lightly. He farts occasionally. There's a lot of noise from outside – cars hooting, rushing past. The light from the window is yellow. I can see the edge of a huge neon *Coca Cola* sign. I feel . . . lonely I guess. Tired.

At the time I didn't recall anything. I ran out of the door and down the stairs, blinking in the bright sunshine. I ran as far as I could, until I was terribly lost. People stared. I washed my hands and shoes, and smeared mud over the bloodstain on my trousers.

I found the nearest road and got a taxi back to the hotel. It was ten past five. Joe was in the kitchen. 'How was your afternoon?' I said.

Now that I can think about it I know exactly what happened. It's in my mind in freeze-frame images. I don't need a hypnotist to release each detail from the deep recesses of memory. Those seconds, from the instant I took that candlestick in my hands; from the instant I felt its weight . . . they're all far, far too clear now.

I close my eyes momentarily. A thousand thoughts go through my head. Am I going to die? Am I going to kill? Have I made the wrong decision? What if there's an explanation? Do I have a choice now? Is it too late?

I think about what I set out to achieve that morning, before all this happened. I wanted to show Joe . . . what? How open minded I was. How mature. How *un*racist, for want of a better word . . . But more than that: I wanted to convince myself that this Egyptian stranger could be trusted. It wasn't just to prove a point. I wanted to learn something for myself. I wanted to become a better person, to become more reasonable, because so many times we go to a foreign country and we treat the people like shit, and we generalise and we stereotype to the extent that we're blind to reality.

I want desperately for this man to be genuine. I want to be able to scold myself for my previous fear and paranoia. I want to prove *myself* wrong, as well as proving Joe wrong.

So have I given the Egyptian enough chance? Do I have a choice now? Should I wait until my own blood splatters the wall before I stop trusting these people?

I open my eyes. I see it now: the first thing to emerge from behind the wall is . . . a tea tray. And there are teacups on it, with chips around their rims. And there's a metal teapot. And there's a sugar bowl. And the tray is covered in a tasteless floral design.

The face emerges. My mind twitches. It knows that something's wrong but it can't work out what. My hands are moving in a wide arc. I feel my muscles releasing their pent-up energy.

The face is . . . smiling.

My arms – the candlestick – come into view. My brain is screaming No no *NO*! but it takes too long for the message to get through. I see the face flicker with surprise. The candlestick hits that exposed nose . . . and it bursts open. The face crumbles. I can hear the cracking of tiny bones. I can hear the gasp of exhaled air. I can hear the squelch of wet flesh.

I drop the candlestick and my legs start to move. My last view? The Egyptian man – my guide, our friend – collapsing, the tray crashing down down down, water spraying outwards, blood pouring into the open hands. I hear his low groan. I grasp at the door handle. I flee.

That's it . . . I can't think of anything else.

That's all.

LINDA ROGERS

Snail Love with Opera

I think of you lying in jail at night
listening to the music you asked us to send,
thinking of her, while Beethoven's only opera,
Fidelio, the heartsick husband in prison,
plays in my head, and snails with soprano
voices make noisy love in our garden.

This is what Mozart meant when he wrote
Eine kleine Nachtmusik, A Little Night Music,
arias sung in flowerbeds, where slippery
inamorata, floating on silent carpets of dew,
make their slow way through the tea roses
and dahlias, forget-me-nots, to dirt
hotels where they twist and twist,
the pyrotechnic friction of flesh
making the holy madrigals of men
and women in love, just like you, all
alone, listening to music in your cell.

Was it Mozart who first called the love
portal of women a theatre? Was he thinking
of Venice, the first opera house, and snails
crawling out of the sea with prisons on their backs,
then filling them up with air, the volatile
mother of water and music and the viscous
fluids exchanged when camerata, the passionate
stories, are sung in gardens where luminous
footprints of snails are songlines
people of genius are compelled to transpose
when the time on the ceiling is almost
dawn, and even the deaf composer, lonely as
the celibate tenor, his candle burnt down,

only one song playing itself over and over
outside his window at night, is able to free
his hero Fidelio from the agony of love with treble
notes so high they can bend prison bars?

This is the sound of hermaphrodites
glowing in the dark, their bodies acquiescing
to the music of grass harps and insect singing,
their lyrics produced from shining orifices
in the face, their opera houses lit up
and the Midnight Express freeing the prisoners
of love, all of them lying awake and listening,
so long as light shines through bars.

TRACY HORN

Homage

I think for England that's what I do, I think for all the infractions
and cadences of reason which is my england. None other.

i think for all the tidal waves and tributaries of Englands plural

On ancient crust of wrist and ankle bone dust
i think for the cream, the comingling of these
the divisions the rulings,
and for steel, i think for steel

I think for all the frail stock of england all satchels making their way
towards schoolhouses on light legs through the brittle charm of our
winter.

i think for you because ilove you. must.

i think for the possibility of future rose gardens
i think for there must be roses.

and paragons of virtue among your weary slaves.

Unwaged i think for england,
on the rock and roll ithink for England
with a special increment for thinking sickness an ocupational
hazard in this game which game the thinking game. I think for
england.

i think therefore the english rascal is hereditary isn't it?
don't we form through blood in Blighty –
from kings to lonely Anna Key? don't we?

and did i hear that builded here a temple
by aching slide and rule and many many hands
and were we not the same, me and thee?
in this temple, no never.
thinking for England, I realised: no never.

i think for england cos bent double on margate sands coughing on wet fags
we survey the waters, heavy from ships rusting inwardly at the core of your seas and every so often a live one grey like a mirage against equivalent skies

my england still at war,
its samely lens still on the darkening page
all is she, all am i. nothing else is.

my subject is England,
i think for it.

CERI ANN WORMAN

Hush

And sometimes there's rain and more rain
A relentless curtain of sound and when it
Stops the silence is more profound by contrast:
Electrified, an anticipation,
Like an audience before the curtain
Poised between this life and the next;
Or as if the world is holding its breath
Counting to ten before it starts again.
Then doors open, children tumble onto wet grass;
Or the curtain rises and the drama begins.
The moment is lost, that hiatus,
But I'm inclined to feel it more and more in things:
The pause before a kiss or after a photo flash –
The illuminated hush that lightning brings.

NIGEL FORDE

Visitors

They are building, this March, between
Eaves and rafters, somewhere in the hot dark;
Haunting the bedroom with feathered sounds.

At morning they are wingbeats in the copper beech,
Wet runes by the water bowl or shadows quietly
Bending to the business of cool gardens.

We cannot name them. Loose in the sun they sing,
But come silently, invisibly, home to roost,
To fidget like stars all night, or soft rain on stones.

Reading in bed, we listen for them now,
As for the door scrape of a daughter safely home;
They peck along the roots of our noisy dreams

In whose half-light we follow ourselves back
Along the uncertain ways of love again,
Through a frost-creak stir of silence, the tiny

Spider's footfall of an egg ticking.
The stealthy quotidian, the sift of our history
That was frail and unrehearsed; that is adequate.

JANE DRAYCOTT

Public Records Office

'If you would see something quite dreadful, go to the enormous palace in the Strand, called Somerset House . . . What can men do in such a catacomb?'
Taine – 'Notes sur l'Angleterre'

Ink comes in on the tide and with the watermen
and moths cuts up the stairs. Witnesses crowd
the courtyard in pairs, details are lost in the rain.

Behind the dead windows darkness is swallowing
the *Aula lucis*, the hall of light, like a sword:
year by year, marriage by marriage, a steady hand.

Last night, another murder in the watergardens.
Torches doused, the facts sit in pools on the flags
and that blind old allegory the Thames refuses to speak.

No mention here of those unaccountably let off
the hook, of the dates they were not with their friends
in the runaway hackneys, the train wrecks

or warships which broke like a biscuit, cordite
gangfiring back like a family tree through torpedo room,
ocean, the North Sea, past sandbanks and home.

In the river, the house and its offices hang like a ship
smeared with soot and the memory of flame underwater.

JAMES MACILRAVIE

'Cause

'Because is a woman's answer'
Shakespeare, *The Taming of the Shrew*

'Cause Mackie, we *bæth ken*
That when God sends that thunderbolt
We neither *i wiz'll* be able
Ti say no

An' è hae ti – mak' the album
Feenish the script, get the degree
Star in the film, *traevel* the world
And then *u'm* free – *ti* settle doon

An' u'm jist tellin yi
'Cause if you touch me
Wi' this pelt and *a'* this health
That's *a' mèh* dreams up in the air

An' è winna be able *ti* say no
'Cause yi'r far too handsome
And *yi* speak *tha'* low
It's like *bein'* rocked *ti* sleep

An' è like *bein'* rocked *ti* sleep

PAULINE STAINER

Eclipse at Skara Brae

There it was –
reflected in the roof
over the Neolithic village,
bloom of salt
on the glass
like a grave-mirror
misting at the breath.

And the dead?
Did they pluck
the daylight-altering herb
during those moments
of lovely dislocation,
and feel time
supple

as one of those
sword-blades
which can be bent back
until the point
almost touches the hilt,
before springing back
undistorted?

REBECCA GOSS

Aeroplanes

I like to think, when the bomb went off
she slipped from her seat
into the sky, floated for a time
before the body broke apart.
It's difficult to keep her whole.

Now that this package has come,
(her things wrapped in plastic)
I worry they were carelessly scooped up.
That I will tear away the wrapping
to find her fingers, loose, like crayons.

Night of the news flash, I sat on the stairs,
absolutely sure she had survived.
I kept my runway of Christmas lights
blinking on the banister for weeks,
but she didn't make it home.

I'd signed for my daughter's things,
went to work, left them untouched in the hall.
Opening my front door now, a stench hovers.
Diesel fuel, instantly thick in my throat,
with the hang of disinfectant behind.

The package mocks me, it's what I've waited for,
but I find it choking, unpleasant.
I lift it to the garden, let the smell seep upwards,
hear the rumble of distant aeroplanes.

Eagerly, I look for her.
The long, hard legs puncturing clouds
as she falls down to me.
My hands getting ready to grab the feet,
pull her safely through the trees.

MARIO PETRUCCI

After School

We were a class of two
with the empty oak pews of learning behind us
and the corridor quiet
while the master ran through the question

and no thwack of willow
dimmed through glass; just light, cramming the lab
the master unknowable in white
pondering the question, the long corridor quiet

till he remarked some aspect
of the answer might have been better dealt with . . .
but the window's brilliance
caught his eye, cauled him from the paper

so I had sense only of the electron
tight in its orbit, that no music from dim transistors
nosed, near-extinct, through the glass – here
was all we could know. Vacant light. An open corridor.

GILL SAXON

The Heart's December

Don't call it love, that isn't what you mean;
I'd call it lust, but that denies your charm.
Don't give me that, just say it straight, come clean
For once and risk it; what can be the harm
In saying something if you know it's true?
Is that it then? That's all you're going to do?
I'm sick of bloody poetry and song!
Life's far too short to sit here listening to you
Spouting, and I'll be dead too long.
Oh love, he cries, *sith Jove hath curs'd thee so*
That Bleak December in thy Heart holds sway
Let Angels weep and flood the Earth below
With melting tears until Spring bringeth May.
She smiles a frozen smile. It starts to snow.

HOWARD WRIGHT

Old Money

Tuning in to the sound of the sea, we get beechtrees in aspic,
and tall light through original windows, and a shadow the size
of the lawn creeping into the village laid out like a picnic
for the side-by-side white cars at-ease with themselves.

Evening. The sound of children destroying the narcissi
and snowberries. Crows creak and croak in the single clotted elm
above frost-blackened palms the invisible gardener has neatly
decapitated. Later, post-prandial, a cafetière in the drawing-room

brings the tongue-tied daughter with a tray of matchless Belleek
to the high fire and jaded magazines, the bright platitudes
painstakingly elevated to clever ideas level with the teak
cornices and gloss pelmets; the congenital attitudes

preserved in sepia formaldehyde like all those dead teams,
devout and self-absorbed, at the back of a maudlin university
quad. And though the Colombian coffee is not what it seems,
it keeps us awake while the owner relates his inadequacy.

For this isn't your normal hotel. No, even the jokes are blue.
The children sleep. The pillows spit out mint chocolate
even as we rip the blankets from a mattress that was never new.
Before breakfast, before dawn, ghosts sit down and wait.

GORDON TAYLOR

Yodelling

arms and arms and arms and in eyes pupils spin the way records do
and o the dizziness I want to sleep but in dreams I speak sign
language I have never learned and the ache that waking makes the
lifting of arms to stretch is a remembering of the body and arms
and arms and arms and o the sound of sewing machine clacks in
the passing of boxcars no one hops off no one jumps on and the sea
in the rush of cars outside my window and the airplanes travelling
low like thunderclap and the breaking of the sound barrier and rain
like applause and the unheard beat of sun like the heart and my
voice and your voice and the sound barrier o the dizziness and the
cough like a seal's bark and every sound seems to echo in some
other and walking near midnight by the lake you tried to imitate a
loon and as you waited for reply I realized I must remember
everything because we are using these sounds to make the next ones

BRIAN CLOVER

My Mother's Cigarettes

Like the wise virgins lying side by side,
straight and white under their silver sheet
when you secretly lift the cardboard lid.
Carefully pull out their chaste silver bed,
feel their various weight,
they roll and titter till you slide them back home.
Butter wouldn't melt, would it?

Or dent your thumb on the stiff case clasp,
open and find, like a lucky giant,
six of them, wasp-waisted by a common belt,
held safe from terror like girls on a 1950s holiday,
strapped into the ferris wheel,
leaning on the promenade rail,
pinned to Wall of Death with toothy smile.

Both pack and case innocent, happy,
though stiff, musty and dry,
as girls would be when oil,
conditioner, lipstick and scent were luxury.
But later, in the pub or dance hall,
they flared dangerously, burned bright,
and bent at last into grey ash.

BRIAN CLOVER

Pushing the Envelope

The school inspectors have been in all week
'Which I don't mind too much, actually,' she says, 'but . . .'

And he has lost a quarter's invoices in their bulldog clip
And tore the place apart . . .

But now he lies on her
Rocking the back of her estate car,
Too many tools and greasy in his van,
Essay file creasing unheeded her bare hip,
She urgent as he and surprised by it,
They fall out of time

As clouds roll off the moon and part
And stars are gleaming in her eyes and in the sky
Like specks of milk on a black cat
Or her deep private sudden Milky Way.

Stars upon stars
Without name
Purpose
Judgement
Paperwork

PAUL LEE

Up the Junction at Fahrenheit 451

His reading age was always older than him:
some books he read were older than both of them.
He'd borrow, buy, read them anyway, for the words –
juicy as the raisins in the puddings his mother made –

with which he'd stud the pewter-plain speech
needed for peers and family. Mocked for his *posh*,
lip curled, he'd ask did they know *precocious?*
then use *staccato* for *intermittent*, and vice-versa.

At puberty, his need to understand words known
to childhood, becomes urgent. He buys Nell Dunn's
bourgeois slummer's novel of urban squalor,
set in Sixties' working-class macho culture,

where no one does drugs or seems to booze.
They fuck furtively. They prefer greasy cafés'
egg and chips, and tea, sweet and stewed.
Its young men are quiffed, in love with speed –

the two-wheeled snarling type – T-shirts,
blue jeans, black leather jackets and boots –
still that Brando thing two decades on.
The story's core is a back street abortion,

knitting needle induced, the foetus wrapped
like fish and chips and flushed down the toilet;
not the knowledge he seeks, but worth a boast
to his brother, who grasses. The book burns, tossed

on the fire by his mother. *Fahrenheit 451*
he thinks. Henry Miller continues his education,
takes him to the *Tropics* and for quiet days in Clichy,
and O, such amazing words, used properly.

VALERIE DARVILLE

The Silver Fish

I was alone all that hot, dry summer.
Too restless to stay indoors I walked and
walked, killing time with motion. I remember
that Sunday was scorching and a brass band

playing in the park by the river. I
walked the long way round. Why not? Time was the
thing I had too much of. The sun, high
overhead beat down remorselessly

with an intense white light. I suppose this
is why the usually dark, dirty
water was pellucid, transparent. Fish –
enormous silver fish – in groups of three

or four, formed circles, noses together,
breaking the surface of the water to
gasp for air. Everywhere along the
bank people marvelled. Blue damsel flies flew

zig-zagging about the river adding
beauty to the scene. Awe and joy touched me –
as if gods had come among us, singing.
I had not known there were so many.

ANNE-MARIE FYFE

Morning on Bridge Street

The new address is lighter than airmail:
on blue my street-name looks faint, watered.
I unwrap my mother's fine-bone chattels,
sugar-bowl crazy with hairline fissures.
In 5 a.m. still, the locals aver
that time hangs slow, conscious of being
a stone's throw from the not-long dead
who thrive on such broken mornings. The blind
accordion player on the bridge hollers
it's the real, the absolute, time of day.
Thanks you for the chink of currency.
Passers-by strain to catch his underplayed
wheeze. The postman abandons his route
in small hours. Residents
listen out for a noiseless whistle.

DENNIS CASLING

Signs

When Jaques Derrida came, we went to hear,
aimless in inarticulate pursuit
of wisdom, dapper in its tie and suit,
that made the ground beneath us disappear –
a sense of disconnection taking root.

My half deaf friend stood up to make a point.
Derrida didn't understand his drift,
and, seeking signs, began to search his face.
They stood in limbo like the desert saints.
I watched Derrida knot his tie and lift
one hand, as if delivering a grace.

MARCY WILLOW

Revelation

Men are like Hattifatteners,
She said. I knew what she meant,
Having read Jansson, though in translation.
She said, The way they mill about,
All tall, with their big eyes.
Those staring big eyes.

We sat on a crusty boulder,
Crumbling blue lichen under our pink heels,
Our toes stretched out over the giddy green sea.

I raised my chin to nod. A cormorant
Swept by, searching the swells that
Shrugged their way toward an island.
Out of the eastern horizon, like a peacock,
A schooner arose, over-masted, it seemed
From our talus-bound viewpoint,
Skerry, really.
And pale, she said. Tall and pale,
And the way they drift around in groups like that.
Bunches of swaying Hattifatteners. She sighed,
And leaned back on her elbows.

I leaned over my knees, and in the blur,
Where blue met green, saw St. James' Park,
A tall, tailored back, suave as the black swan.

Can you stand it?
She was saying.
What?
That finger-waggling.
Why do they do that? Fluttering fingers,

And mumbling. Only they know
What they are saying. She flopped back and
Dropped onto her face a handkerchief,
Quite frayed.

Wings akimbo, the cormorant stood
Bedraggled by useless plunges.
Beyond, the island waited for the schooner,
Its scalp of firs prickling.
The lichen, with symbiotic stubbornness,
Clung to their granite cushion.
I rubbed at their impression on my thighs, tracing
In the maze, the way to the stone footbridge,
Turn of shoulders, gaze of grey
An embrace light as a mist-net.

Suddenly there they are. Close-ranked,
Mumbling, or silent, I don't know
Which is worse. Your hair stands on end,
Not surprising – Yes, I remember –
It's their electricity. They show up
Looking for thunderstorms, and leave
In a flotilla of messages set adrift. Sailing
Away in those little round boats.

For a while, she read, I began a letter.
The whisperings of pages and pen-point
Were soon only those of pages.
On the parapet, a hand opens,
Down long fingers roll the last of the petits fours,
Cake crumbs tumbling to the hopeful ducks.
I wonder what it's like in a coracle,
I said. That's how they come.
Who?
Hattifatteners, I said.

SIAN HUGHES

Sex Education

The week before Options they put three science sets in one lab
and switched off all the lights. Those who giggled at the cartoon
were sent outside, and had to grow up not knowing about sperm.

KAZ SUKS was carved into the workbench deep enough to read
with a finger in the dark. Gary Foreshaw chewed paper pellets
and flicked them at my neck to show he didn't care about breasts.

The teachers stood together by the door, and whispered.
One of them had to get to the bank at lunchtime.
How about a lift? Could no one find a window pole?

They read out all the worst mistakes in our written tests
and said they were amazed. 'We have no choice
but to put you all down for a D in Reproduction.'

My fingernails were full of gum from the ledge under my seat.
Someone turned on the gas taps and pretended to pass out.

KATHRYN KULPA

Los Gatos Bus

The husband and the wife didn't quite match. He wore jeans and a light-brown tweed jacket and a white oxford shirt. She wore jeans and a pumpkin-coloured t-shirt and a dark-brown tweed jacket she'd taken off and draped over the back of her orange bus-station chair. They both had their weekend bags tucked under their chairs, peeking out between their feet. They both looked tired. He handed her a bottle of spring water and she took a sip and handed it back.

'Maybe we should have had it towed,' she said.

'No, if they can make it drivable I'll ask Jack to run me down tomorrow, and I'll drive it back—maybe he knows a good garage—but if it is the transmission, I don't know that we'll want to put more money into it.'

'Can we afford a new car?'

He had a sip of water. 'I was thinking more a . . . not-so-old car. Not quite so old.' He handed the bottle back to her and she took it, mouthing a silent *thanks*. She drank and held the bottle to her cheek. She laid her hand across his, palm down. She would have sat closer to him if she could have. He would have sat closer to her. But the Greyhound bus depot in Santa Cruz, California, was not built for intimacy. Its chairs were hard plastic, moulded, a little dip for the bum like bucket seats in 1970s automobiles, and bolted to a thick beam of steel, so that nobody could move his seat too close to another person's, or too far apart.

Across from the husband and wife an old woman in a furry black velvet hat was blowing bubbles through a wand. 'Look at my butterfly bubbles!' she said. 'They're magic bubbles, you know. If you make a wish on just the right bubble it'll go straight to the eyes of God, straight to heaven, and you'll get your wish.'

Two children stood next to her, brother and sister, clearly: same pale eyes and almost albino hair, the girl's in a thin ponytail, the boy's short as toothbrush bristles. He frowned and pushed against the girl with his body. She pushed him back, closer to the old woman.

'You could wish that you would turn into a butterfly, and then you would.' Loose skin bounced under the woman's chin when she talked. She wore a black coat with a velvet collar, though the day was warm for October, and a jewelled butterfly pin.

'I like monarch butterflies,' the boy said. 'Did you know they fly to South America in the winter? It's called migration.'

His sister stepped on his foot. 'My brother wants to know if he can have his bubbles back,' she said.

The wife was looking at the children. 'I wonder who they belong to?' she said. The husband glanced around the room with the air of someone who seldom notices other people unless asked to. There were a few youngish white women, a ginger-haired man with mutton-chop sideburns, some college students, a Latino family with a baby in a carrier. The old woman winked at him and sent a bubble his way. He turned back to his wife.

'God, I'm sorry about this.'

'Why are you sorry?'

'This mess of a weekend. I'm sure you didn't expect to spend all of today in a garage and a bus station.'

'It's not your fault the car died,' she said.

'It's not only that. If we have to buy a car I don't see how we can go away this Christmas break.' The husband reached in his jacket pocket, glanced up, saw a sign–*We Care About Your Health NO SMOKING*—and took his hand out of his pocket with a sigh. The boy ran past him with a shrill, shrieking laugh, followed by the girl, and he winced.

'So we'll go next year. Or the year after. I don't mind.'

'Hardly a honeymoon.'

'Why should people have to take a honeymoon the same year they get married? It's conventional,' the wife said. She nudged his arm with the water bottle.

'A thirty-year mortgage!' he burst out. 'What was I thinking?'

'Sweetie, nobody rents around here. It's too impossible. In San Francisco four or five people are chipping in to buy two-bedroom condos.' She tilted her head to the side. 'What's the matter?'

'Nothing. Just me—an old tube of gloom as usual.' He gave a small smile. 'Never did get around to those papers, did you?'

'Oh, God. I can't stand to look at them.'

'Like me to do half?'

'They're ESL and remedial freshmen. You'd pull your hair out.'

'No, really. I don't mind.'

With a doubtful look she reached into a canvas tote bag and pulled out a folder of papers, handing half to him. 'Be kind,' she said. She took out a red pen, and, starting to read, traced the blunt end absently along the outline of her lips. The woman in the velvet hat watched her.

'There's character in a face,' she said. 'Well shaped, well defined lips: the sign of a generous nature.'

The wife smiled a little, hesitantly, and looked down at her papers.

'Freckles are of the blessed,' she said. 'A sprinkling of gold from angels' wings. Freckles are a gift from God, a sign of virginity.'

The husband raised his eyebrows at this information. He smiled at his wife. 'You see? That sunblock will do you no good, my dear. They're a gift from God.'

She scrunched her nose up at him. The woman turned her attention to the husband.

'A long nose indicates pride,' she said. She reached into a plastic shopping bag and pulled out some yarn and a pink knitted square.

'Oh, there's something to this, I think,' said the wife.

'Perhaps Mme Defarge would like to measure the bumps on my head to see if I'm a criminal type,' said the husband.

'Pride goeth before a fall,' quoted the woman, as if to no one in particular, and started to knit. She looked up when she heard the wife laugh.

'He's really very sweet,' the younger woman said.

'Am not *sweet*,' the husband muttered. Now the old woman was watching them intently.

'You've got worries,' she said. 'Money troubles. Never worry. The Lord will provide.' She glanced upward, as if that money might come floating down from heaven any moment. She nodded.

'Before the year is out. I'm seeing green around you: the colour of money.'

'We'll have to play the Lotto then, won't we?' the husband said, looking less annoyed than he had.

'We'll buy a brand-new car,' the wife said.

'Take that trip.'

'Pay off the mortgage.'

'A long trip.'

The wife, tilting her head back, drank the last of the water. 'Why am I so dry today?' she said. 'My mouth feels parched.' She took a pot of lip balm from her purse, dipped in her index finger, and ran it over her lips. She gave a quick smile to the woman in velvet, who was watching her.

'Lips like peonies,' the woman said in a dreaming voice. 'But paint them—I say paint them if you want the smell, but paint tells tales, yes it does. Many a young woman has been saved from committing adultery by a good lipstick.'

The wife pressed her lips together in a half-smile. The husband crossed his legs, slipped on his glasses, clicked a pen open on his knee, and bent to his reading with a determined air.

'It's good for the man to be a little older,' the old woman said. 'I think so. We last longer, ladies do, but if you're a little younger, then when the hubby dies you're not too old to catch another man. That's what happened to me. I was seventy-two years old and my Frankie dropped down dead at the breakfast table.'

'I can see you're still dumbstruck with grief,' the husband muttered.

The wife poked him in the thigh. 'I'm very sorry,' she said.

'That's all right. But don't worry, dear. Your man's still got a few miles left in him.'

Rather grimly the husband slashed out several lines on the paper he was reading. The old woman looked up. The children were blowing bubbles. The wife touched her husband's hand.

'I'll call Jack and Zoë and see if they can pick us up at the bus station.'

He nodded and slashed out several more lines. But he looked up and watched her walk across the depot until she rounded the corner where the pay phone was and the lines of his face, held in a kind of half-amused, disbelieving disgust, softened. The woman in the velvet hat also watched the wife walk away. She looked at the husband.

'She's lovely,' the old woman said.

The husband nodded. 'She is.'

'Poor girl,' the old woman said. 'She won't live long.'

The husband sat very still.

'The black. It's on her. I thought it was on you but it's on her . . . blood. The poor girl. The poor, poor girl . . .'

'Shut up,' he said. The children turned to look at him. He stood up, stuffing papers into bags, snatching up his wife's jacket. 'Leave us alone,' he told the old woman in a savage whisper. She stood up and put a hand on his arm as he started to leave.

'I don't ask for them,' she whispered. 'I never want them to come.'

The husband jerked his arm away. 'Don't look at her and don't talk to her. You're a filthy—bloody-minded old—leave us alone.'

He went and sat in the farthest corner of the room. He pulled some papers out and held them in front of him, leaning forward, elbow resting on his knee. The papers shook. He held them but his eyes looked in the direction his wife had gone. He saw again that *We Care About Your Health! NO SMOKING* sign. The prohibition against smoking was repeated in Spanish and Chinese, but apparently the management only cared about his health in English.

He saw his wife coming around the corner and waved to her. She looked puzzled but nodded, walking his way, and a young black-haired man in a leather jacket approached her, putting a hand in his pocket. The husband stood up. He called her name. She looked at him and waved. The young man held out a dollar bill. The wife nodded and took some coins from her purse. The husband sat down.

'I saw you,' she told him, sitting down beside him.

'I know.'

'Why'd you move?'

'The crazy woman. She kept babbling . . . I couldn't think.' His voice sounded false and too loud. The wife frowned.

'She probably has something wrong with her . . . Are you all right? Are you hot?' She touched his cheek.

He took off his jacket. 'Too much sun.'

The sun was behind her, casting a copper glow over her brown hair. She handed him a fresh bottle of water. 'I got Zoë,' she said. 'They're going to meet us. I thought we could go out for a drink.'

'Good idea,' said the husband. He gazed across the room. The old woman in velvet was staring at him with a ridiculously sad look on her face; he turned away. Meanwhile the PA system was crackling.

The wife stood up. The husband didn't. 'Hey,' she said. 'It's our bus.'

'*She's* not getting on the bus—!'

The wife shook her head and half-smiled. 'Did she tell you you were going to be Thane of Cawdor?'

'God, don't quote that play—!'

'Why are you so twitchy?' She looked up from her bags. 'Oh, come on, you're not—that stupid thing she said—'

'What?'

'The lipstick. And committing adultery. You know I'd never . . . I mean . . . you do know, don't you?'

He nodded slowly, and stood up at last.

'I mean, sweetie, I picked you. You know that. Right?'

'I do. I am humbled every day by that knowledge.' He smiled and picked up her weekend bag. 'Let's go.'

'Hey.' She followed him as he walked towards the bus. 'Lose something?' She handed him a scratched, bulging attaché case. He took it and looked at her.

'I'd lose everything without you,' he said. 'You know that.'

'Sure,' she said. 'It's nice to hear a man admit it.'

The blond girl and boy were shoving each other, both with a foot on the first step of the bus. The man with the mutton-chop sideburns hooked a finger into the boy's collar, and the girl sprang up, crying 'Ha!' The husband stayed back, watching his wife get on the bus, watching her feet on the steps.

She stopped at a seat, seven seats down from the velvet woman. 'Okay?'

He nodded.

'You'd better sit on the end. Your poor legs will be all squashed.'

She was right; the seats were cramped. He stretched one leg out into the aisle. 'No more grumbling,' he said. 'Promise.'

She put her hand on his and braided her fingers over and under his. 'Secret handshake?' he asked.

She shook her head. 'Not secret. My mom and I used to do it in church when I was a kid. You know, when we weren't supposed to talk.'

'And what did it mean?'

'It meant—not mad. Love you.'

The husband turned his hand palm up so that her fingers came unlaced. He folded her hand together and covered it with his own. He looked out the window. The city had gone by.

'Los Gatos next stop,' the bus driver announced.

'Los Gatos.' the old woman said. 'That means, the gates.'

He could see the heads of the two blond children, probably kneeling in their seats, looking at the old woman who sat behind them. He looked away.

'The gates of heaven,' she said. 'There's a story about that. Los Gatos, the gates of heaven. One day there was a prince, and he loved a princess—the most beautiful princess he had ever seen, and her name was—'

'Tracy!' said the girl.

'Tracy's not a *princess* name,' the boy said disgustedly.

'Well, it could have been,' the woman said. 'Yes, I think just maybe it was Tracy—and she was very kind and good.'

'And *beau*-ti-ful,' said the girl.

'Yes, she was. And so one day the Lord took her up to heaven to live with him, and she was very happy there. But the prince who loved her was angry. He was so angry! He yelled and cursed and did terrible things.'

The husband's sunburned face grew redder.

'Then one day he decided that he would walk and walk to the end of the earth. He would walk until he found the gates of heaven, and he would smash them down—'

'Los Gatos means the cats, man.'

The husband turned around. It was the young man in the leather jacket who'd asked his wife for change.

'Not some gate of heaven bullshit. Los Gatos is cats.'

The old woman was silent.

'He's right,' the wife told her husband. 'It does mean the cats.'

'I don't like that story,' the little girl said. 'Tell a story about kittycats.'

'And she was wrong about the lipstick, too,' the wife said.

'Cats,' he said.

'Cats.'

She smiled, a big brilliant smile. She would smile that way when she told their friends about it. She would hold a glass of wine and laugh. The husband would laugh, too. He would refill his glass and stare into its dark red and tell himself that they had met a mad old woman who told extravagant lies and whose Spanish was worse than his, and now he would forget her. He would tell himself that he would not see broken glass and smashed metal each time his wife got into a car, or the knife in the stranger's hand when she walked. He would not think Keats with every cough, or with every blue mood Sylvia Plath, and that night when her breasts filled his hands he would not feel for the unfamiliar thickening under the skin. He was an educated man and not a medieval peasant and he did not believe his destiny was mapped in the stars or the Kabbalah or the tarot pack. He did not believe the truth lay in blind hermits or sheep's entrails or weird sisters upon a blasted heath.

Still he looked out the windows of the bus at fields that had been green but now looked brown and bare, and long after his wife had lost herself in the pages of a book his own lay open to the same page and he looked out at the highway like someone whose hard journey lies ahead, like a man stranded on the roadside thinking about the long walk home.

LESLEY BYERS

The Way to a Man's Heart

My name is Guiseppe Brancuso and I am a fat and happy man but I will tell you the story of how once I was thin and a soul in torment. All my life I have sold meat. Oh, not meat like the Tinacci brothers who have the stall next to mine – not the red, hard cylinders of fillet and brisket trussed up with string or the sharp, bony arches of ribs and haunches of hogs, no, I am a specialist in the delicate parts of beasts.

Thirty years I've been in the business, my father with me and before me, back three generations since we gave up trying to grub a living from the pitiless Sicilian soil. My father saw to it that we had one of the best positions in the market so that even in midsummer the marble keeps us cool and the meat fresh. Of course the market hall in Palermo is famous, a temple to trade, a theatre, a circus for rich and poor.

The fishmongers are on the left, we are on the right. The smell of meat and fish, both good in their own way, do not mix and so we are separated by the other stalls, vegetables, dry goods, cheeses. Opposite me for example are the Morelli sisters, fine, handsome women with a display to match. You want olives? Do you want them in brine or the finest olive oil, black, green, dried or plump? Do you want them stuffed with pistachios, almonds, anchovies from Trapani, red or green pimientos or chillies, loose, bottled or pounded to a paste? Go on – choose – they will have it! Think of a fruit, candied, dried or rolled in sugar, the finest, the most intensely sweet you will find there. Indeed their display has been photographed. Yes, I promise! A photographer, a real one mind you all in black, with a shiny metal suitcase full of cameras, came to take pictures for a magazine. Can you believe that some people will buy a magazine to look at pictures of food? He was from Milan of course.

Tourists are always taking photos in the market, of the hall and the stalls, mine included. The ceiling is high and vaulted, like

Tinacci's racks of ribs and the tiles and mosaics are magnificent though when you work here all the time you don't see them any more, if you understand me.

The tourists never buy anything. Oh, perhaps a peach or pear to have with their lunches. Well, I say lunches, they sit on walls outside or benches in the park and nibble bits and pieces out of paper bags – not what we would call lunch. To us they seem strange people, large and pale like the fat round a spring lamb's kidney. They wander around whispering to one another, pointing, making themselves small against the noise, the smells, the sights.

They tell me there are no markets in these northern countries, just quiet, shiny supermarkets where food is sold in little pots and bags and trays covered in plastic. Bah! I tell you these people creep about as if they're afraid we'll eat them. We wouldn't of course, too stringy, too bland. Don't look like that – I'm only joking!

I'm well known here and well liked though I say it in all humility. For a long time, my fellow traders were all the family I had. My motto is 'Every customer is a stranger but once.'

Take Signorina Clemenza now, she is the housekeeper to Professor Lupino and his wife and that lump of a son of theirs. She reminds me of a hen, small, buxom, fluffy, she picks her way through the market as if it were a farmyard, her eyes glittering like chips of jet, her little beaky nose pointing and sniffing. We know our lines, it's like a game of cards or a fencing match.

'Good day to you, Signorina, what will meet with your approval today?'

Her smile is like lightning, a flash then it's gone. She walks to and fro, she looks at the liver, the kidneys, the sweetbreads, the brains, never goes beyond the brains does Signorina Clemenza. My opening gambit:

'How were the kidneys received?'

'The Professor praised them to the skies,' she boasts. I made a 'ragu' of red wine with onions and herbs and served them on a cushion of rice.'

I kiss my fingertips and congratulate her and counter with:

'Perhaps lambs' liver today then,' I suggest artlessly, showing her the dish of soft, ruby slices. I always slice – so much more refined.

'Grilled, brushed with oil, a little oregano maybe?' I know she'll raise the stakes not to be outdone.

'Calves' liver!' she chirrups emphatically, 'sautéed in butter!' Another lightning smile.

I feign astonishment.

'Inspirational!' I declare, 'with sage, a squeeze of lemon – perfection!'

I see a flash of irritation on her face – she has to concede the sage but ripostes with:

'Not lemon juice, no, lime!' she says triumphantly.

'Always a refinement from Signorina Clemenza,' I sigh, shaking my head in wonder.

Then I have my next little joke. I take one, two, three, four, creamy slices of my best 'fegato di vitello', silken between my fingers, fanning them out on the waxed paper and look at her expectantly.

'Mm,' she deliberates, 'another two slices I think, they're not so large and they do shrink in the pan, you know.'

I nod deferentially and add the slice for her niece and the slice for the niece's husband. Employers know that this goes on I think.

Then Signorina Campina drifts by like a wraith. Forty years of housekeeping for Father Patrizio has turned her the colour of a tombstone. There was always talk about those two, years ago naturally, always will be where priests and housekeepers are concerned for are we not all still men and women whatever the clothes we wear? Now she frets about keeping him going, for what will become of her when he is gone?

She dithers and mutters and I catch the words 'cod' and 'steamed'. I step in.

'Look at these sweetbreads,' I say, peeling off the membrane to show their freshness. 'Now, gently poached with a thread of vinegar, pounded with a little salt and pepper, rolled in white breadcrumbs and fried in good oil – ambrosia!'

She recoils in horror. Did I say 'poached in arsenic' perhaps or 'roll in broken glass'? Did I, crazed with lechery, pinch the old girl's skinny arse? No, I did not. I said 'fried' and she shrinks from me as if I were the devil himself.

I rescue the situation. Boiled calves' feet were the good Father's penance last week, this week's is to be tripe. I choose a piece of the finest, as white as a starched surplice, soft and woolly as a sheepskin between my fingers. I have heard, I tell her, that the French would cut it in spoon-sized pieces and stew it in milk with an onion and a scrape of nutmeg.

'Lazarus himself would come back for that,' I assure her.

She almost laughs and I wonder whether she will cross herself to atone for my irreverence.

It was just after that that SHE appeared. I don't claim to recognise everyone who comes to the market but she was new, I would have remembered her. She was looking at the beef on Tinacci's stall and Fabrizio was flirting with her. He can't help himself, with that man it's an affliction. She stared him down, raising one eyebrow and giving him a 'drop dead' and no come-back. She walked in my direction. I forced myself not to stare, pretending to be busy and gave her a respectful 'Buon giorno.'

She asks for chicken livers and I think maybe she has a cold, her voice is low and husky. I ask whether she plans to make a paté. She is silent for a while then, not looking at me, replies.

'No, I think I'll dust them in seasoned flour, fry them, add Marsala to the pan and when the sauce is thick, throw in some green grapes and serve it on crostini.'

I gape. I close my mouth. A vision and an alchemist! As I give her the change I look for a wedding ring, don't see one and say a 'Grazie mille signorina.' She doesn't contradict me. Then she thanks me and our eyes meet. Que ochi! Huge, brown, pale as the finest calves' liver steeped in milk. I watch her go, what a woman! She is tall, broad, not fat you understand, straight like a queen, hair thick and curly like a crown.

'Hey, Guiseppe – bet you'd like to get your hands on that – a real piece of meat for a change.'

It was Fabrizio, calling over to me and slapping his hand on the chunk of rump he was cutting. Buffoon. Idiot. Moron. What can you expect from a butcher, the soul of a poet?

That evening I stayed in. I cooked myself 'fegatini di pollo in Marsala' savouring each morsel, imagining the green grapes passing her lips, the taste of the wine on her tongue. I was jumpy, I couldn't settle. Perhaps I would go down to the café and watch the match, no. I didn't want to be with people. My head felt light, my skin itchy. I wasn't tired, I couldn't read, there was rubbish on the television. Then, staring at the ceiling, I saw a smudge I hadn't noticed before. I got a chair, climbed up and to my horror saw it was a great, black cobweb. Disgusting. Then I saw furry stuff on top of the curtains and as I touched it, it crumbled into a shower of dust. I was horrified. I was mystified. How had it got there?

I found a cloth under the sink. It was stiff but I soaked it and tried to clean the cobweb and dust away but the water ran down my arm and I only made it worse because now there was a black mark on the ceiling and the curtain was wet as well as dirty. Bewildered, I went through the apartment and discovered that everything was dirty. Stunned, I sat and thought it through.

It had been four years since Anna had died and although I could use the washing machine and changed my bed-linen when I remembered and always washed my plate and glass at night and my cup in the morning, I had done nothing else. To tell the truth, I had no idea that anything else needed doing. Had Anna cleaned when I was out of the house? She must have done. How were things cleaned anyway? I had no idea. I had been living like a bear in a cave for four years and I was ashamed.

Now I'm a practical man and I've always said that if you can read, you can find the answer to most things so I searched out one of Anna's books, the one my mother had given her before we got married. It was called 'The Young Wife's Guide to Housekeeping'. You can't imagine the trouble that book caused, Anna's mother nearly called off the wedding she was so insulted. Hadn't her daughter been thoroughly taught and properly raised da da, da da . . .? Anyway, this book made it absolutely clear what had to be dusted, what had to be washed and scraped and scoured and beaten and, best of all, how to do it.

You would have laughed! Out of the cupboards came the cloths and brooms and buckets and the feathery dusters on sticks and I began, working like a demon till I fell into bed.

She didn't appear the next day and, to be honest, I was glad because I thought I was getting the 'flu. The strange buzzing in my head was still there, I was perspiring a lot, my heart was going like a trotting horse and I had no appetite. It didn't affect my work however and that night, armed with bleaches and powders and polishes and creams I carried on my cleaning. As I worked, I began to notice things. They'd always been there but I'd stopped seeing them. For example, why dust all these ornaments? They meant nothing to me, had no value sentimental or financial. Why wash all the mats and doilies which covered every surface? They weren't beautiful, I don't think they were useful. No, there was a great deal that I would just parcel up and give away.

I began to look critically at the apartment. The wallpaper was brown and flowery and when, I ask you, are flowers brown? Only when they're dead, that's when. The curtains matched it and clean or dirty, they offended me. I would paint everywhere, everything would be bright and new.

That weekend, despite my 'flu symptoms, I painted the apartment, from floor to ceiling, sideways forwards and back till it looked like new. It was barer, lighter and a little bit strange. I cleared cupboards too and parcelled up all Anna's clothes which still hung like moths in the wardrobe. Poor Anna, may her soul rest in peace, I loved her and was as good a husband as I knew how but it was not a joyous marriage – she was born to suffer and bleed and there was never a child to comfort her.

On Sunday night I was exhausted and filthy and whilst drying myself after a soak in the bath, I caught sight of myself in the mirror. At once, all my enthusiasm and resolve drained away like blood down a sluice. Once I had been handsome – surely I had been handsome – so who was this grey, lumpy, pitiful creature before me? I got angry, a good powerful anger and swore that I would change myself, after all do we not hold our fate in our own two hands? I was only forty-two, no age for a man, full of health and energy and, if you'll pardon me, the forces that make a man.

I would visit Paolo the barber, he would change my hair, trim my moustache, he would tell me where to buy new clothes, I would spend a little money, no, a lot of money! I would make trips and get the sun on my skin.

A week later you wouldn't have known me, in fact, I hardly knew myself, I was smarter, straighter and thinner, too, what with all that hard work and my loss of appetite.

Then she appeared again, straight out of my head and my dreams. She was talking to Lucia Morelli and my body, which I had punished so much, got its revenge. My mouth dried, my heart thumped and my legs turned to tripe.

I can't remember our conversation, only that she would have lambs' kidneys and cook them in white wine and mustard and that she smiled at me, the splendour of her eyes enveloping me like an eiderdown.

The thunderbolt had struck – I was in love, as bad as a mortal can be. How long did I gaze after her, mesmerised by the rocking of those magnificent hips, hips you could build a dynasty on? No more than ten seconds I suppose but a man can dream a lifetime in ten seconds. I had named her, wooed her, wedded her and bedded her, christened our children and worshipped her white hair. Yes, there would be children, a son of course, to carry on from me and witness I had lived by his name, but a daughter, please God a daughter, now that would be the real thing. She would be tall and noble like her mother, proud but modest, too, and when the time came I would set her up as a father should and give her a wedding which would make Palermo gape.

She reaches the corner and I tell myself that if she looks back, I can hope. If not PAF! – that's it, I'll go behind the counter and cut my wrists. I tell you I was a crazy man.

She's at the Rossetti stall. She stops. She picks up an orange and half turns her head. Then she looks across and smiles, not the smile of a flirt, you understand, but one of warmth and complicity. My life is saved.

That night I ate kidneys in white wine and mustard sauce, stared at my newly-painted walls and drove myself mad. Go on, laugh, I can laugh at myself now but at the time I was in torment. I didn't know how to speak to her, what to say, how to declare myself. It had been over twenty years since I had courted a woman and then I had been just a boy on a Vespa chasing the girls and it had all seemed so easy.

And now be patient for my tale is almost told. Twice more she came, twice more we chatted about nothing that mattered, how thin I had become, was I well, twice more my courage failed me. Then came the day.

Her mood was different, purposeful, brisk even. She seemed impatient with the pauses in our conversation. She didn't know what to choose and rejected all my suggestions. She walked the length of the counter, reaching out now and then to adjust one of the earthenware dishes. Then she stopped. She was looking at the dish of testicles. I was paralysed.

With a long look at me, she reached down and and picked up a pair in her one wide hand, testing them, weighing them. She arched one black eyebrow and, fixing me with those luminous eyes said, very softly and slowly:

'I think I'd like these, but I'm not sure what to do with them – are you going to tell me Guiseppe Brancuso.'

Carlotta and I were married five months later. Two years after our marriage, she gave birth to our children, Guiseppe and Laura, the names I had chosen that day in the market hall. She is, and always will be, the most beautiful woman and the best cook in Palermo.

My name is Guiseppe Brancuso and I am seventy years old and though I have lived a life full of happiness yet I think that this day is the happiest of all. Carlotta has just left for the church on the arm of our son and in a moment I too will leave and on my arm will be my Laura, my bellissima Laura, radiant in white.

MIKE CASEY

Securex

Larry lets the last executive out of the Henderson building into the frozen street and tips his peaked cap.

'G'night, Sir.' He politely ushers him out, controlling the flourish of relief in his voice and hands. Because of the snow there will be no overtime, no stragglers; in fact most of the staff had left even before he came on duty at six p.m. It's a clean sweep; the building is his for the night.

He locks the revolving doors, drawing the cylindrical cowls around, snapping home the bolts. The entrances are like pressure chambers now, sealed tight as a drum. The security cameras slung from the cantilevered first floor point their barrels at the entrances to make assurance doubly sure. The Henderson is secured for the night.

The snarl of traffic dies; the smoked glass of the building turns the neon galaxies and the cruel frost-laden wind into memories. All that is hostile is outside, partitioned; there is safety inside. Even his sinecured breathing is drawn into purring ducts and pasteurised. Yet although he is well bunkered in, there is an air of nervous expectancy in his stomach, because nothing is ever that predictable.

Keys jangle on his belt as he walks back through the brooding lobby. Fourteen paces bring him to the nearest elevator, metallic doors sliding open on cue. Must remember to put the clock back – or is it forward? – tonight. Diane will know. Six-thirty. It begins.

Riding down to the security console below ground, he smells perfume in the elevator. His middle-aged featureless face, split unevenly across a triptych of mirror panels, queries this; it is usually cigar smoke.

'Locked up?' Diane looks up briefly from the bank of monitors, two for each side of the building. Her heavy black face under the uniform cap has an indigo tint from the screens and an air of grievance.

'Just saw the last one out,' he says with satisfaction. The perfume has given way to what can only be steak and onions.

'It must be freezing out there. City could be snow-bound tomorrow.' She moves heavily towards the small adjoining kitchen.

'I wonder.' His eyes dwell on the question . . .

Seven p.m: As usual Diane keeps the larger, leaner steak for herself. But it's not an issue because Larry likes fat especially when it's crispy and sweet and sort of explodes in the mouth. He mops up the gravy with a soft white roll.

'Eleven goddam hours to go,' Diane grumbles, 'and I missed Oprah again.' The steak has not settled her; eaten bread is soon forgotten. She may not be cut out for this job which must, Larry knows, be taken a minute at a time and not projected too far out into the void. He has known others like her who never learnt how to abide in the moment, who spent their time fidgeting and looking for distractions. *Unresolved discontent* was what the shrinks called it.

As she finishes the evening paper which sustained her for only fifteen minutes, she pushes it towards him commenting, 'Gas explosion on Sixty-Fifth Street.' She knows this is the only item that will interest him.

He scans the column briefly: a couple of casualties but fortunately no buildings damaged. He makes a large pot of coffee, one cup each every two hours, sensing Bob and Lil watching him out of little pink eyes.

'Keep an eye on the screens.' Diane pushes herself away from the console. He looks at the eight internal windows focused on points where the city glances off the Henderson; these tangents can be revealing. You never know what the camera lens will fish up through the scum.

She feeds Bob and Lil, the two fail-safe hamsters kept to monitor the air quality. After eating, Bob scampers back through the plastic maze to his little treadmill while Lil was quivering nose drinks from a thimble fixed to the bars of the hutch. They vouch for the atmosphere.

'Wasn't it my turn to feed them?' Larry asks.

'That's OK.' Misunderstanding, she makes a compliment of it.

For her, everything about the job is a chore even if done willingly; that's the difference between them.

He points to screen five where, amid the real and electronic snow, a human figure can be seen crawling at the bottom of the steps near the rear entrance.

'Yeah, I saw him earlier.' Diane nods. 'Booze maybe, or drugs. Who knows?' Her sigh implies that nothing out there comes as a surprise but that fact in itself is an enormity. Her lips fold over the striped straw protruding from the giant beaker of coke – a Big Gulp – making the crushed ice rattle against the waxed paper.

'Maybe he got mugged?' Larry offers. They'd seen a rape on screen a couple of weeks ago. It is impossible to exaggerate the chaos out there.

'Could be.' Her eyes wander over the other screens set side by side like a comic strip, then back to screen five where the action is. Maybe this cameo will occupy her for a while, give her the distraction she needs.

Eight p.m: In the express elevator lined on all sides by mirrors, he notices how his many reflections taper off to a yellow dot and then nothing although it can't be nothing. The touch-sensitive buttons almost read his mind and the elevator launches him to the top floor to do his rounds.

Pacing the corridors, he has a view of the other buildings that rise above the city to a rarer level, tall enough to be trusted. Like the Henderson these are the named élite: the Chrysler, Empire, Negresco, Liberty, Citicorp. Do they acknowledge each other across the empty spaces? Are they somehow part of the same family, like peaks in the same mountain range?

As he skirts the perimeter it occurs to him that the more time he spends in the Henderson the longer he will live. He cannot be hurt in here; it is a life support machine, an incubator for adults. Although sometimes, just once in a while, he has the vaguest unsettling sense that it could all explode, as if the white noise is the hissing of a fuse already lit.

The open-plan spaces he passes are filled with desks, filing cabinets, blank screens and pampered plants. He notices how some of the individual work areas are personalised with calendars, posters, macramé pot holders, and others not. He wonders what really goes on here when the Henderson houses its staff, wearing its other unobtrusive face. He might have known once when he started out and thought the job was beneath him because it was only minding a building which was impregnable anyway. But now the idea of security has become an end in itself and it isn't necessary to know what the end product is. A monument doesn't have to justify its existence; that's all he has to understand.

From the charge of static when he touches a wall and the reassurance he feels when he lays his cheek against a polished granite pillar, he can tell that the Henderson is alive. He regrets the years he spent trying to understand what it did instead of feeling what it was.

Falcon-like he circles each floor, then drops to the one below. On the twentieth he unplugs a photo-copying machine which was left on, and notices, on the glass panel, a sheet of crumpled paper which reads: '. . . has had several warnings. The operational side cannot carry Mr. Gaffney any longer.' So, they'd finally caught up with that maverick, Gaffney. He deserves to be fired. His office is a mess, the carpet like a Swiss cheese from cigarette burns, especially near the settee where he sometimes crashes after a night on the town. He just uses the Henderson in his comings and goings. Maybe he's a PR man or something but, still, he should show more respect. Larry doesn't know what to do with the crumpled page so he just leaves it where it was, wondering why he has been led to it.

At the console Diane has turned to her project for the union, designing a work roster that will increase overtime. She is always looking for an edge or an angle, driven to this not just for the money but because it is a sort of therapy which nurses her through the long hours that she makes longer by wishing away.

'If we can get into them for time and a half on the early week-end shift, that might make a case for double time on the night shift. It might work. Hmmm.' She pushes her papers and charts aside, knowing he is not interested. 'There's a hell of a lot of responsibility in this job,' she adds, supporting her case. 'More than they give us credit for. The damn building alone is worth what . . . five hundred million bucks? Easily.' His silence makes her more aggressive. 'And what about all the top secret stuff they keep here? If any of that got out . . . . They just don't appreciate what we do here . . .' She stops abruptly, realising he is dumb enough to like the job, and is the sort of wimp the union can well do without.

'What top secret stuff?' he asks innocently, not meaning to call her bluff.

'All of it. Don't you know anything?' All that classified material . . . . They don't pay us for securing that. Or for the goddam boredom. It makes me sick.' Looking at screen three she sees a young man relieving himself against the side of the building. 'Pig! Five thousand volts up the whang would soon teach that punk.'

Larry nods grimly; on some things they can agree. But he wants to change the subject because he's never seen her so agitated. Maybe the void is beckoning to her. 'How's the other guy? Number five?'

'See for yourself.' The crawling figure has reached the steps and lies face down like a crouching dog, limbs bent awkwardly under him. He seems to be etched in black because the snow has melted in a narrow strip around him. If there is body heat he may still be alive.

'Is there nothing we can . . .?'

'No.' She cuts across him and shuffles a pack of cards. 'Want a hand?'

'I don't think so.'

She deals for solitaire, thinking it was a mistake to have eaten so early, thereby leaving too much time on the wrong side of that divide. But the steaks had looked so good . . . .

Ten p.m: Towards the end of this tour Larry drops into the boardroom on the twenty-fifth floor. The table set with decanters, leather-tooled pads, gavel and sounding block, is as big and shiny as an ice rink. The empty chairs surrounding the table give the impression of a mystery pending, of strange words yet to be spoken. It is a good room for whatever goes on here; it is presumably the control centre where ideas are transmuted into decisions. The brain of the building. Whereas Larry's little console room below ground is the heart which sends him trouble-shooting through the veins. The thought pleases him until he notices the portraits of cold-eyed founders glaring from the walls. These images are wrong, out of character; the hard flinty faces undermine him. He touches his forehead against a panoramic window and despite the referred vibration of the wind outside, becomes calm.

'He's almost had it, I think,' Diane says when he returns to base.

'Bob . . .?' He looks in alarm to the hamster's hutch.

'No. Number five. Maybe he was stabbed. That dark patch, there, in the snow. Could be blood.' She points to the screen with a ringed finger.

'Could be.' It's not easy to tell; the fixed-frame screen does not oblige with a close-up.

'Or maybe he odeed after all.' She changes her mind peering at the tube. 'It's not a great reception.'

'Can we not . . . do something . . .?' Because his loyalties are divided he feels confused. Decisions were never his strong suit and this job has so far spared him from tough choices.

'And leave our posts? Anyway it *could* be a set-up.'

'You reckon?'

'You never can tell, not for sure. Why take a risk? Any risk. There's no percentage in it. Our job is tough enough as it is.' She bridles a bit and her hair which curls up under the navy cap in tight kinks, beginning to go grey as if singed, seems to quiver like live fuse wire.

Larry is relieved she's put it so well, so strongly; it absolves him. Security has to be all or nothing, no half measures. If you stray once beyond the limits then it all becomes uncertain; once you walk out there the door slams behind you. The very thought unnerves him. It is Diane's turn to pour the coffee . . . .

Midnight: This time he goes straight to the middle floor and the middle stall in the bathroom. It's not that it's different to the other stalls but he's used to it. On this level, too, there is good water pressure; one flush is always enough. He feels good here in the innermost Chinese box, right dead centre, at the very core. They can't touch him here. Ha! they can't even find him. He is hidden in a childhood dream, though far from lost.

Outside, a ceiling light flickers in distress about to blow out. Mysteriously it will be fixed tomorrow night. Maybe, in the reflected power of its efficient sheen, the Henderson can heal itself. But what if the opposite is true? He must be vigilant, alert to the possibility of self-sabotage.

'Is our friend still there?' Larry asks. 'On five.'

'Uhuh. He moved a bit more. But I think he's cashing in now. Why does it have to happen on my watch?' Implacable, she turns the diversion into a chore; she has never learnt the secret of waiting.

Larry cranes towards the screen until he feels the down on his face tingle. There is indeed a finality about the proneness of the figure, a dispirited yielding up; the snow is beginning to move in as the blood temperature falls, spreading its crumpled white winding sheet over him. What a difference, Larry thinks, between being in and out, a life of difference, and only a wall separates him from nurturing warmth, but that's how it is.

'It's a question of territory,' Diane says loudly in justification. 'If he made it to the entrance and buzzed it might be different, more official. *Then* we might be able to take a hand; we would be responding to a call. Know what I mean? It wouldn't be our *initiative*. See? But I doubt if he'll make it that far.' She shifts in her chair; the end of her spine, despite its mammoth insulation, aches from prolonged sitting.

Again she has cleared it up for Larry, putting the rightness of her case beyond doubt. His mother was forceful like that, able to make up his mind for him by laying down the law with a clarity that defied objection. But still some sinewy instinct of his own prompts him to ask, 'What if we . . . called an ambulance?'

'I thought about that. But we'd be in a mess then. Cops, questions, maybe even accusations. It's not on. We've too much to handle here as it is.'

He welcomes this assurance. Anyway the reception on screen five is not good; a vague second-hand relay filtered through lens and tube, grainy as an old photograph, does not give the certainty needed for action.

Diane opens a brown paper bag and offers to trade a ham on rye for a pastrami. After their early-hours snack they give crumbs to the hamsters still thriving on the recycled air. Soon after this unscheduled feast the hamsters sleep in their straw litters and happily remain breathing. There is nothing sick about this building.

Four a.m: he rides down to the underground car-park which is empty except for Gaffney's battered pimpmobile. So, Gaffney is on the town again. Odd that an intelligent man should want to throw it all away. Judging from the memo Larry found, it looks like he's succeeding too. Should he warn him? Of course not. Diane would laugh at the suggestion and anyway why should he pass on the secrets the Henderson offers to him after hours? And of course Gaffney doesn't know him from Adam although he's passed by him often enough. It's not a sore point; a good security man *should* be invisible, shadowy behind dark perspex, a mere presence hidden in a giant presence.

There's a Gaffney in every building. Before the Henderson, Larry had worked in the Rowantree. The maverick there had caused a fire one night that blew out the electrics. Larry had seen the screens go blank and almost lost his reason. He was blind for several minutes, exposed like raw flesh. He never wanted to be caught like that again. No, he doesn't have much sympathy for mavericks and shit-disturbers. One is all you need to wreck the whole system. This Gaffney can take his lumps.

Passing by the public counter on the second floor, he sees the sign for couriers: *Helmets must be removed when approaching the counter.* Under it someone has scrawled in magic marker, *Fuck off.* The public are uncouth, not to be trusted at all; they bring the grime of the outside in on their shoes. Signs on. The carpets here are soiled and worn, the wood panelling stained by nicotine and greasy heads and hands. The Henderson is ageing badly on this floor. Although the damage is localised it is still worrying because it shows, no, it proves what can happen. The Henderson does not wear people well, public or staff; it shrinks from them, withdraws into its shell, its antibodies fighting to reject the foreign matter.

Larry stays for a long time on this injured floor as if sitting with a patient in a quiet hospital ward. Tonight the closeness is special. He is running his hands gently along the battered public counter when Diane bleeps him: 'There's a Mr. Gaffney at the front entrance. He wants in but he's stewed.'

Larry rushes down to the console and assesses the situation on screen one. Gaffney is swaying slightly and trying his best to run on the spot for warmth. It is clear that he wants to get in to his office to sleep if off.

'I guess you'd better let him in,' Diane says.

Fear spurts through Larry. The moment has come sooner that expected. He croaks into the mouthpiece, 'We don't open till seven.'

'Let me in, Goddam you,' Gaffney shouts back, his voice gravelly over the intercom.

'Go home. Get a cab.' Larry quakes at his own barking sounds; there is no going back now.

'There's a dead body out here. Open the fucking door.'

'I'm sorry.' There is something of Diane's confidence in his utterly new voice.

'For Christ's sake . . . .'

'I'm sorry.' He discovers a whole new sound range. An inflection of regret can actually stiffen the message.

'You'll hear about this, whatever your name is.' Gaffney shuffles off through the snow muttering, 'Fucking cretins.'

Diane looks in surprise at Larry whose heart is beginning to recover a more normal beat. 'We could have stretched a point. He is staff after all.'

'Huh, he's no better than the public. They're all the same.' Larry is still stunned by what he's done and by the feelings that are pouring out of his mouth. It is liberating in a way but he also knows that he has set out on a long road. It starts snowing heavily. Currents of wind from the side of the building whip the snow into flurries, dispersing its force.

'That guy did croak by the way.' Diane points to the screen. There is a long white blanket of snow covering the body; the ridge looks like a pauper's grave. She shudders. 'This job sometimes gives me the creeps. I can't wait to get home.' As she looks at the brightening screens which light her face with the promise of a new day and the next shift, she seems to have been drained by the night.

'Home?' He smiles in surprise and sympathy. As the morning continues to seep into the screens, now the colour of oyster, he goes on tilt again, knowing that assertiveness will not come easy, that it will cost him more each time. Waiting with a purpose is not the same as just waiting. It is chilling how quickly time passes now, relentlessly, because it has become a prelude to action. So this is what they call tension? Was that its seed all along, in the white noise, the hissing fuse, the silence at the heart's core, the infinite reflection in the elevator? Though he'd missed these omens it was too late to back out now.

At seven some of the staff assemble angrily on the front steps stamping their wet feet, rubber-necking in disbelief like hounds that have lost the scent. He watches them on screens one and two, looking for some redeeming sign. The buzzers sound angrily. The hamsters wake and rattle the bars of their cage. The intercom is glutted with sounds of outrage.

'Larry, go and open up! What's the matter with you?' Diane is already in her street clothes, dressed for freedom.

The sick dread has given way to that midnight calm. 'No.' He rests his face against a pillar.

DODIE ELLIS

Still Lives

Thursday afternoon is Art Class. Held every week at the Unitarian Hall in Galton. Galton used to be a village before the town swallowed it. There's a dusty Co-op with a few dead flies in the window and an assistant that used to know everyone. The one-way system is a way to get round the clutter of parked cars in streets made for bikes and horses. Everyone in Galton has 2.2 cars as well as kids. The Unitarian Chapel below the Hall has a mural that attracts visitors from abroad. I've only encountered Americans. Every week I drive from the heart of the town to have a three-hour break in another life. I come early to grab the window seat, well away from the Still Life and Edna. Not everyone can distinguish between them. The Hall is standard pre-war issue: chilly, badly lit, paraffin fumes, though the fire is electric. The class is held in the Upper Room – awkward for heaving kit, and the kitchen and water are downstairs. We're like the disciples waiting for the Holy Ghost. On sunny days gold dust freckles the air and lands on scrubbed floorboards. The other forty-eight weeks – it's grubby and dark. Today is typical November.

In four years I've learnt how to hold a brush and can confirm that watercolour is a difficult medium. I know more than I let on about complementary colours, golden triangles and perspective. It doesn't show in my work. If this was football my intentions would be to kick a ball around and have a giggle, not to win the Cup. Actually I come to take up where I left off at Mixed Infants thirty-five years ago, and to forget I am on the Supply Teachers List and may be summoned at any time to Criminal Park Middle School. Trying to be creative makes me feel better about myself.

I have sold my soul to the L.E.A. for a mess of pension but my dream is to write. So far I'm experiencing writer's block without ever having written. I had hoped the Art Group would act like an enema. I was sure there'd be enough undercurrents and seething passions to sink the *Titanic*. So far it's Lake Placid. Nothing more than a grandchild's disappointing GCSE's results to dimple the surface. It is great for unhampered ear-wigging and observing nuances of behaviour. For example – last year's Monet exhibition at the Royal Academy: some had their lives turned round by this, others wouldn't go two yards because of the queues, and then there was Edna. Edna thought that Monet could learn a thing or two at her easel.

The tutor is very patient. Week after week he keeps doing the rounds. He explains nicely where we are going wrong, where the light should fall, where the vanishing point should be, continues on his rounds, and returns to find we have pursued our own wayward paths. He's a proper artist. He must long to snap brushes, flick murky water, kick some butt. At four o'clock he swiftly packs away cabbages, grapes, busts and urns, while we draw it out, basking in Bohemian ambience, hanging on in there to the last dregs, even if that means scraping pastels off the floor. He says his aim is to make us look. He quotes Ruskin to the effect that plenty can talk and think, few can see. On the drive home I often do feel as if a skin's been peeled from my eyes. The countryside rises up to meet me in green gobfulls. The flip side is – I notice how grotty my kitchen has become when I walk through the door.

This particular Thursday Rembrandt at the National is the hot topic. The tutor has been twice and been inspired. Not many others have bothered. Rembrandt doesn't have the pulling power of Monet. Audrey went but spent more time in Harrods buying a babygro for her new grandson. Edna's been. Edna goes to everything and is yet to be impressed, 'Two hundred self-portraits. It wasn't as if he was anything to look at. If I looked like that I'd have stuck with apples. It was a relief to get into the shop.'

Faye is opposite me as usual. She usually does cheerful pastels. She's just heard her midwifery teacher has been put in a home. 'I wish I could be half the midwife she was.' I would have killed to have Faye present at my nemesis. She wears these luscious Indian prints and shoulder-tickling earrings. Sitting opposite her is like a winter break in Goa. I can't imagine her in uniform. Her family make mine look like guests on *Rikki Lake*. Her daughters ask her to go to films with them. Debbie scoots into shop doorways if she sees anyone she knows when we're out together. Faye is making plums look delectable without a six-inch crumble topping. She has almost convinced me it's normal for Debs to be scraping up two inches of hair, rolling her eyes, and calling me 'Mother' with attitude. She distributes nose-bags of re-assurance. Occasionally I want to tell her about Minna. For years I told everyone who said more than three nice words to me. When I found I couldn't talk it out I gave up. Anyway – Faye must hear too much of that in her job. Not everyone gets handed into the car with a lacy shawl.

The room is hushed with concentration before the ongoing tea/coffee rota feud kicks in. I push to one side – Faye's side – the watercolour I've been overworking of Heyford Church and flick through possibilities at the back of my Langton pad. I use 140 pound paper because I'm too slothful to stretch. I pull out a sketch pre-dating Edna's run-in with the vicar over Roy's cremation. (That enlivened many a Thursday.) The drawing was based on an advert for a classical music cassette, 'Relax with the Greats'. It was a chocolate-box country lane overhung by back-lit leaves. My picture is going the way of oh-so-many other bland designs.

The tutor is wrestling to pull Edna's 'Yacht on Coniston' back from 'Unidentified Object on Unidentified Substance'. She grudgingly hands over her Kolinsky Sable. She has every brush from emulsioning barn walls to two hairs – swordliners, hakes, hog fans, riggers. The inside of the Gucci hold-all feels like Marilyn Monroe's mink. She snaps at the tutor, 'Careful. I've already got the frame.' Her bungalow walls are difficult to find. In local exhibitions her pictures get pole position. Mine get hung so low down my only following is among dachshunds. That grievance stirs up something in me.

I dump my cheapo Chinese brush and plunge into the gunge at the bottom of my carrier. I find a fluff-encrusted big no-fuss brush. (The one I'd simply had to have and then never used.) I am determined to abandon my itsy bitsy style, swiping tasteful colours off the palette with what's left of my sponge. I got the palette free with five artist quality tubes. The sponge resembles what's left in the water after a piranha attack. But I am not deflected by any of this. I work up a rainbow of pure pigments, some of which are near mummified. BLACK? I didn't know I had black. Watercolourists treat black like the media treated Paula Yates. I boldly daub where I had only dabbed before.

I don't hear Irene's first call for a show of hands for tea of coffee. Beverage time has much in common with hustings. Irene gets between me and my masterpiece to get my order. I would agree to arsenic. Irene's perfume is bringing tears to my eyes. Irene volunteers too often. Most people keep their heads well below the parapet until someone else cracks. The kitchen would freeze an Inuit. Funny how Edna's name never reaches the top on the rota. Irene comments. 'There's bold. Reminds me of my kingfisher tablelamp on the telly. Ernie likes his telly. He's piled on the weight since he retired. He looks like a hairy blancmange. I watch more lamp than telly.'

Edna is hot on her heels, like a rottweiller after a buttered poodle. 'What are you on? You must be knocking back the water tablets. There isn't a bird in sight.' She jabs her brush handle at my shoulderblade, 'What are you copying that from? Wouldn't want that on my wall. Give me nightmares. Death. That's what that is.' The cream expanse of Berketex is snow-blinding me. She wears a different pastel outfit every week with toning accessories. Her hair is the most natural blond known to hairdresser.

The tutor doesn't investigate immediately. We'd spoken at some length about Heyford Church at the outset. Everyone must get their fair crack with teacher or else petty jealousies arise and rumours of clandestine liaisons circulate. Brittany currently. He is fair game – under fifty and known to paint nude women convincingly. Edna is easily diverted by a waft of jewellery party tickets. Cloche Gildonne – tacky but expensive.

Faye peers over my shoulder, on tiptoe, 'That's really good! Not like anything you've ever done before.' She didn't mean it to sound that way. 'Don't interrupt the flow. I'll fetch your tea. I see it now – birth. The miracle of birth.' I don't have the heart to tell her I've been drinking coffee for four years. There's usually one cup astray. Edna probably jumps choices to keep us on a creative edge. My picture is no longer the advert, that much is clear. I muse, sucking my paintbrush. I hope Winsor and Newton don't contain lead concentrates. I feel guilty not getting my own drink. Like when I had chicken pox and my mother came in everyday from cleaning offices, struggled up the stairs with a tray and I only had five spots. I also feel embarrassed. The painting feels too good.

The lane isn't chocolate box, more like somewhere a rapist could lurk. Distant black trees arching overhead with clawed hands, foreground trees great rounds of emerald life. The path shifts and swerves like swallows. Maybe that's where Irene got the bird image. I can see a foetal shape, circled by curving lines. The tutor murmurs, 'Did you known you've done a Madonna and Child abstraction?' What do you think? One thing I do know – for the first time I've painted an image I couldn't explain better in three words. I try out titles, 'Every birth a splendour. Birth song of the sea.' So far I've only produced work entitled 'Autumn in Chipping Sodham' and 'Heyford Winter'. I think I might settle for 'Lane to the sea.' No sea in evidence, but I feel it's round the bend. Or maybe I am.

The socialising is in full swing. Valerie surreptitiously wipes her teaspoon on the back of her pencil pleats. Her allergies are in full swing. She's got Irene pinioned. She's had to cancel a bargain break in Suffolk because the hotel couldn't guarantee 'clean'. She makes Walberswick sound like Beirut. Apparently Jim was glad because he knew she wouldn't sleep for worrying about her mother. 'It comes back on me at night. Someone has to make sure they're doing the job right. That place isn't cheap.' The staff have begged her to take her mother for Christmas. 'But what if she falls down? She'll only make a fuss about going back. I think I'll bring her fire tidy in for the Still Life next week. We've had her coal fire replaced with gas. Less dust. The fuss she'd make if she saw that. I'm like father. He never liked Christmas.'

Irene manages to get in a word, 'Me and Ernie don't make much of Christmas or New Year, being as how we're on our own. New Year I don't cook till late. That puts the time on. If I manage to put off the washing up while half past ten, we don't have too long to wait. It's such a long haul otherwise.'

Valerie says, 'Father hated Christmas. He always said, "Another one over." Edna pipes up, 'Your allergies are all in the mind. My mother used to be pally with your mother, Mavis. She said she was so nervy your Dad threatened to have her put away. You take after her – not Albert.' Valerie blows her nose and knots her burgundy silk scarf tightly. No prize for guessing whose neck she's imagining. At school Valerie was cross-country champion three years running. She brings her inhaler to the class in a sterile pouch.

Derrick the Tax Man is telling Faye about his Tesco socks. He hadn't worn them above five times when they went holy. Luckily he can still wear them around the house. He can hardly feel the holes, and what did it matter anyhow now he's retired to spend more time with his wife? Faye is the only one that doesn't avoid him. His wife's in a hospice. People don't know what to say. Even Faye is inching towards Audrey's group. Audrey's daughter recently gave birth to a ten-pounder. Most people are congratulatory. Edna says, 'They were all that size in my day. Too many puny babies are encouraged to live nowadays. If they do survive there's summat up with them.' I settle back in my shawl of dust. Faye's voice is unusually sharp, but the words are lost on me.

As empty mugs are placed on the tin tray, Faye tries to discharge bad vibes by describing her Adini outfit from Bohemia, a shop in the Mall that smells of incense and Derrick's socks. Their cottons are as silky as my breasts used to be. Edna graciously enquires how much it cost, and didn't her husband mind? Audrey laughs, 'Ted never notices what I wear.' Faye's partner would notice. She doesn't flaunt her good fortune. It's barely six months since Edna's husband escaped to the Crem. He left her well-provided for. She'll never have to squeeze a tube to the bottom. Faye has that secret sex-life glow. For her partner her breasts obviously embody the silver apples of the moon.

Edna graces me with a royal visit en passant. 'That's an improvement.' I haven't touched the picture since she last saw it. 'It reminds me of the lane Roy and I used to cycle down just after the war.' I don't ask which war. 'The hedges were full of dog roses and the grass was right up. I couldn't get the grass stains off my cotton frock afterwards.' She whispers, 'Afterwards it used to sting like bill-io but I liked being wanted. He used to call me "Smiler". If it hadn't been for chips he'd be here today. I heard him remark to an acquaintance once, "Chips are my one pleasure." A Channel Four documentary last week said it takes three and a half hours to bury a body. He'd be damn sight quicker because of the fat on him. Better than being buried. Three tons of earth on top of you. I know what that feels like. Fancy being buried in the earth looking exactly as you were. I went to talk to him in the Chapel of Rest. I always had plenty to say to him. I was interested in everything about him. He never laughed in Cary Grant movies. I should have known then. I had to dab my eyes when we went with the crowd. I gave up going because of him. He said it would all come round on the telly. He didn't like me painting – said it was a waste of money. His sister, Shirley, wanted me to go with her to the Spiritualist over Far Cotton, to contact him. All that way to hear him say, "How much was that blouse?" He said I was excessively fond of personal adornment. He made a mint of money from shoes. Worked his way up from holding rows of tacks in his lips to owning the factory. He must have swallowed so many, it's a wonder the urn doesn't rattle. When we got our Susan's uniform for the Grammar he said, "How much did that cost?" She was heartbroken. He was already a wealthy man. I don't know why he had to try and take away people's pride in themselves. She lives away now. Robert's more like him. Specially now he's thinning on top and thickening everywhere else. I did him a portrait of his golden retriever. He seemed suited, but it's not on the wall. Sharon has a mirror over the fireplace. The young expect you to come to terms quickly at our age. Brian's started sitting next to me at bridge suppers, even when there's other spaces.' She pats her blonde coiffure, 'Wouldn't mind walking down that lane with him.' She lowers her sciatic back onto her seat. She's hardly spoken to me before. I can't believe her nick-name was 'Smiler'.

Another hour to go. To avoid tinkering, I take an interest in other people's work. Most don't bother with what's going on in the rest of the room. Picasso would go largely unnoticed here. Audrey always walks around. But Audrey's good. Her washes are as transparent as her motivation. 'Mirror mirror on the wall, are my paintings still best of all?' The flower table's good for ten minutes. Fragile peonies and roses in summer. I hold Audrey's autumn leaf study up to my nose. I can smell November in the wood. Molly's brown leaves draggle over the page like dog doos. Nowadays her daughter has to collect and drop her. Molly says the same thing every week, about Archie, her terrier. Audrey's got adept at handling her. At the start of class she says, 'Did you have a dog, Molly? Did he go on your bed and spoil your quilt? And what did the vet say when he put him to sleep?' I heard Audrey say to Irene, 'Once we've got that out of the way, she's no trouble. All the life Molly's had – six kids – and only blooming Archie's stuck.'

Margaret's autumn twigs look like a bunch of broom handles with bobble hats. I tell her how well she's getting along. Beginners needs encouragement. More to the point – the hall price escalates termly and we need every fee we can muster.

Brittany hasn't turned up again. She paints Georgia O'Keefe-style full frontal flowers that could attract kerb crawlers. Brittany's a decade younger than Faye and I, and we're the nearest. She wears lilac and oyster camisole tops. They peek out from under her sweats. This isn't lost on the tutor. He spends plenty of time with her. Then she is going through a bad patch. She's separated from Tony with two kids under three. She used to have this top job at Barclaycard. Tony used to check her underwear drawer when she went on business trips. At the finish he used to escort her to the toilet when they went up the Squirrels in Duston. She has trouble getting sitters. Her mother's no help. She wants Brittany to get back with Tony because he's a systems analyst.

I leave a few minutes early to avoid getting stuck with the dirty-water slop bucket. Leaving sounds like the Walton's goodnight routine. It's foggy and dusky outside. I hope Charlotte's driving carefully. Debbie gets a lift with her on Thursdays. Fuel for the EVERYONE HAS LESSONS THE SECOND THEY ARE SEVENTEEN campaign. Mike said it won't hurt to wait till next summer when she can fund herself and she won't have modules to worry about. That goes down well. I stay out of it. She is doubly precious because of Minna, and I have to be doubly careful.

Debs has been in two minutes when I pull up, and has managed to munch the carrots I was saving for the casserole. Why can't she stuff toast and crisps like Stewart next door? The answer is calories. She knows the calorific content of licking an avocado stone. The good thing about her slimness is there's no way she can borrow my things, unless she needs a tent for the Glastonbury Festival. Still, she's come a long way from weighing less than a bag of sugar. I'm dying to show her my painting. She crunches celery, 'What the hell is that? I like it.' I turn my picture the right way round and give her another stab at it. 'Nice contrast. Good line. What happened to your usual cruddy colours? It reminds me of somewhere . . . . You ought to do more of this angsty menopausal stuff. Get it out.' She rushes off to phone Charlotte. She hasn't seen her since being dropped ten minutes ago. I set about preparing supper for the two of us, and for Mike to microwave. He said eight.

It's nearer nine when he gets back and he's in no mood for low-cal lasagne. I scramble him eggs and mushrooms. I leave off buttering the toast, remembering Chip-Face Roy and Ernie the Hairy Blancmange. Mike can't fail to notice my painting. I've propped it on the worktop to be dramatically lit by under cupboard florescence. Will it be 'Nice' or 'Pretty good'? Mike's not exactly Melvin Bragg. He swigs coffee. 'The Lane. After all these years. Did you do it from a photo? You got it right.' And he means RIGHT. He's an accountant. As soon as he says it, possibly a second before, I know it. We'd left there when Debbie was three. The lane did lead to the sea. That's too grand sounding. It wasn't Cornish soaring sea. It was a little muddy track that led to a steely shoreline near Hayling Bridge. I used to walk down there everyday when I was expecting the twins. We lived in an ordinary house but the street had this extraordinary back lane exit. Like C S Lewis's wardrobe. Blackberries, glistening rose hips, a dip where cans and Mars wrappers collected. The spermy smell of sea insinuating along the track. The final corner where the sea showed itself.

I set it aside to give full attention to the high finance cut and thrust world of Wangler Electronics. This is closely followed by the minefield of Debbie's sleep-over at Charlotte's for the party on Saturday. The party is being held at a house nearer to us. Pointing this out causes much 'Oh-mumming' and 'EVERYBODY else is sleeping over'. Mike asks her to name three parents who have agreed. The names sound iffy to me. Unless there's been a flood of foreigners into the sixth form.

First thing Friday morning I turn down the chance of a day at Fidget Park Middle School. Hard to believe I know. I want to be alone with Mike's word processor. I want to get down something about the Art Group. Edna and Faye were both right about my picture. That first evening when we wheeled the resplendent jumbo cord pram down the lane. It was a see-saw time for me. I fretted all the way that the lane was too bumpy. Mike refused to lift the pram over the bumps. I snatched her up, carrying her like she was a glass rose. I wonder if the tutor knows how fragile some of us are. As fragile as the brittle leaves in the Still Life. The serious attention he pays to our struggles is almost like being loved. That room is a golden triangle in quite a few lives. I hope he does take up with Brittany. Next week I'll suggest everyone takes turns at ten-minute poses. It'll give him the chance to goggle her legitimately. She'll stand out – flanked by acres of pencil pleats.

DOMINI STALLINGS

The Broken Bird

My sister Esther told me there were people buried in the wall that circled the bay. She said that if you got too close their spirits could get in through your ears and make you mad. Grandmother said they were casualties from the war when there had been labour camps and we were almost beaten. 'Just think how close they got,' she said, before she remembered to reassure us. 'But it's only a tale, a story.' And she would tell us a potted history of the island; of how it had broken off from France and floated away, and the English had taken it, and that in the war the Germans had stamped right over it.

We came every summer while our mother stayed on the mainland and worked herself to the bone. She had to work because Dad had left and there wasn't any money. 'He could be anywhere,' Grandma said, 'gallivanting around.' And I imagined his waving from anywhere in his best, pressed suit.

Our grandmother's house looked out over the bay and from our bedroom windows we could see a crescent of stone and sand, and sometimes when it was clear we could see the sea. Grandma said to be careful of the sea, that even if it looked calm you could get sucked under and be swept out by the current. She said that if you leave your footprints behind you, the water wells up and washes them away, as though you had never been there.

A causeway ran across the bay to a fort on an island of rocks. Grandma said not to walk out over the causeway because the sea could cut you off, and the fort was old and dangerous, and a mad old woman lived there. We climbed the dunes to the beach where we sank and slipped in the sand, and played soldiers. 'You have to die when I shoot you,' Esther said, 'and you have to scream.' But I thought it would be bad luck. 'Let's play another game,' I said.

Every night as we lay in bed and shut our eyes tightly on the darkness, the windows that were our eyes looked back at us. 'Who's there?' we would whisper. But when we turned on the light and looked into them, we could see only our reflections. 'Who's there?' they mouthed back at us.

It was often cold and wet, even in summer, and we could feel the clouds sticking to our clothes and skin. We searched for shells in the sand and let the wind and the rain blow our hair in our eyes until we could barely see the way forward. Sometimes it was so foggy that the sea was hidden and the sand seemed to stretch away before us without ever reaching the water. But we could still hear it lapping and Esther said that soldiers were coming. 'Can you hear them?' she said. I thought she was silly, but when the lighthouse circled its light like a search lamp, and the fog-horn started blowing like somebody wailing, I said I was going home.

Then we were happy to have grandmother fussing over us, and the smell of the musty moth balls on her woollen dress when she pressed our faces against her hips. 'Your poor mother,' she said, when we didn't wash our hands before supper, or when we didn't eat our greens. And we imagined her working very hard in the city while we did whatever we pleased. 'She never had a moment's peace,' Grandma said to the neighbours, and I thought I saw them frowning.

When we didn't feel like going far we would sit on the back doorstep and watch the people go by, guessing whether Grandma would greet them. We could tell by the way they brushed their hair, the stiffness of their clothes and the shininess of their shoes. She'll never even nod at him,' Esther said, 'she'll never even blink her eyes,' and she was right.

When we saw the mad old woman coming we smiled secretly at each other and waited. She came every day, throwing bird seed from her bag, and Grandma frowned as she walked past and looked up at her windows. 'Don't go near those dirty birds,' she said. They were big and white with orange beaks and black beady eyes, and they balanced on the currents of the wind and they cried like the sea, 'I'm coming, I'm going, I'm coming, I'm going.' 'Yes Grandma,' we said, and she smiled and patted our heads.

Esther thought that the people buried in the wall had filled in the gaps so that our homes would be saved from the sea. It was like in the fairy tale. She said that once she had seen a finger sticking out from a crack and that maybe that's how it all started, with a finger, then a hand, then an arm, and that it had taken whole bodies to stop the water breaking right through the wall. But Grandma said they weren't heroes, they were Russians.

On the road into the village we often found dead birds. Grandma told us not to touch them, but I would wait behind and push them to one side with my feet, and try to rub the blood out of the sand.

'Stop dallying, Ruthie,' Grandma said.

'Why did they die, Grandma?' I asked.

'Somebody knocked them down,' she said.

'Who was it Grandma?'

'Could've been anyone,' she said, and she wrapped her coat tighter round her chest. I thought of the blood in the sand and I washed my shoes in the puddles.

'You can help me clean the church,' Grandma said, as we came into the village, 'Your good deed for the day,' and we rubbed Grandma's polish into the pews with old rags. The woman arranging the flowers said that we had lovely biblical names and gave us her spare change, and she and Grandma talked in soft voices so that we couldn't hear what they said. But Grandma nodded in our direction, and the flower woman looked round and she nodded, too. 'Take care,' she called, as we were leaving.

As Grandma dead-headed the geraniums in the garden, we watched the people go by, and waited for the mad old woman. We could see the fort in the distance and the birds flying overhead and perching all over the roof. 'She must be very brave,' Esther said, 'not to mind the sea and the wind whishing round her, and the ghosts.' But Grandma overheard her and told her not to talk about things she didn't understand. The old woman didn't pass by that day and we kept watching the birds massing at the fort and I remembered the blood that had turned the sand red.

Grandma said we should do something to scare off the birds and stop them eating her berries, so we made a scarecrow by stuffing some of Grandad's old clothes with hay, and tying knots where his feet and hands would have been, and using his hat for a head. While we were fixing it onto a pole, I looked up and saw her. She was standing right by the gate and she was staring. Grandma had her back to her and Esther was looking on the ground for a nail. I looked away but when I looked back she was still staring. Then she spread her arms like our scarecrow and flapped them up and down in the air, and she opened her mouth and smiled a horrible smile, and I could see the gaps in her teeth. 'Pay attention Ruth', Grandma said, and when she finally looked round the old woman had turned and was walking away, with her head bent forward, muttering to herself. Grandma went back to her work.

'She's mad,' Esther said.

'That's because she's full of sin,' Grandma said. She was going to say something else but there was a great thud and a crack and a squawk, and we all stopped and looked round but we couldn't see anything. Grandma told us to go inside, so I was the first to see it lying on the floor with its feathers puffed out and its heart beating through its chest, and its black beady eyes staring. When it saw me it squawked again and tried to fly, but one of its wings dragged down by its side.

Grandma walked through the door and looked pale. 'Get it out of the house,' she said.

'Look Grandma, it's a seagull,' I said. It must have lost its way and come in through the window.'

Grandma looked at the crack in the glass where the bird had thrown itself in wild panic. She sat down. 'Get it out of the house.'

'But look, it's hurt,' I said.

'I don't . . .' She drew in a deep breath. 'Get it out.'

I picked it up in both hands and felt the thin boned wings, like fingers. I kept my hands firmly clasped around its warm body, and I felt it move up and down, up and down, like a heart beating. I walked past Grandma and she turned her head and flinched when she heard its low brooding murmur.

'Bury it in the sand,' Grandma said.

'But it's not dead,' I said.

'You've got to be cruel to be kind,' she said, and she clasped the arms of the chair with her hands and leaned back and shut her eyes.

Grandma said she couldn't stand birds in the house. Their

flapping wings and black beady eyes made her feel trapped, but it made me feel the vastness of the sky, and I shivered.

I carried it outside and sat on the back door-step and cradled it in my lap. I looked through the half-open doorway and Grandma was still sitting in the chair. Across the bay I could see the birds massing over the fort. 'The old woman feeds the birds,' I said.

'What about the tide?' Esther said, but the sky was clear and we could see the sand stretching out before us, and a thin band of blue at the horizon. 'We could bury it,' she said, but I could feel its heart beating, beat, beat.

'Are you coming or not?' I said, and she followed me.

The causeway was old and cracked like the wall and I could feel it hot under my feet, and I imagined it crumbling away beneath me. Esther clasped her arm round my elbow. 'What about Grandma?' she said, but I was listening to the sea and the seagulls calling, 'I'm coming, I'm going, I'm coming, I'm going.'

The fort floated on the horizon like a ship at sea. The water rose and fell around it so that it almost looked like it was moving. As we came closer what had seemed like gentle whooshes of water, to and fro, to and fro, were thunderous waves that pounded against the rocks and sprayed up against the walls, and swelled to twice their size before rushing out to sea again.

The fort looked derelict and as though it might sink at any moment. There was no-one in sight and the windows were broken and covered in barbed wire. The big wooden gates were lying half open and we stood in the doorway and peered into the large, open courtyard. It was overrun with weeds, and in the soldiers' quarters we could see trees branching through windows and pools of water like rain.

Esther saw her first. She had her back to us and was bent double with a shovel by her feet. Next to it there was a pile of weeds. Their roots were torn and wasted, but everywhere you looked more were growing. We didn't move. She stood upright and stretched. When she turned round she opened her mouth and threw her hands out in the air, and flapped them up and down.

'I'm going home,' Esther said.

'I think it's broken its wing,' I called out, but my voice didn't carry into the courtyard. The old woman stared. Esther tugged at my sleeve. 'We only wanted to know what to do,' I said. The bird's heart was barely beating and the old woman was still staring. 'It doesn't matter,' I said, and I turned to go. I thought I heard the old woman calling, but I didn't stop. I put the bird down in a patch of yellowed grass and started walking away. The water was rising and we could see the sand being swallowed up ahead of us. The bright summer sky was growing hazy and the fog was obscuring the bay. 'I wish the wind would blow it away,' I said. But the air had grown still. I felt water seeping into my shoes and I looked down and saw the water spilling over the causeway. 'We're too late,' Esther said, and we started running. The causeway was longer than we remembered it, and I was relieved when I felt the slight incline upwards onto the beach. We jumped down onto the sand and turned back and we could see the fort sinking into the sea.

'Wherever have you been?' Grandma said, when we walked into the kitchen, leaving wet puddles behind us from our sodden feet. She was laying the table. 'Clean yourselves up,' she said, and she looked hard at me. 'I told you to be careful of the sea,' she said.

'Dad would've known what to do,' I said, and I imagined him taking the bird in his hands.

Grandma snorted. 'Where is he then?' she said, and we sat and ate in silence.

We looked for the mad old woman after that but we didn't see her go by. We didn't mention the bird again, and when we walked into the village with Grandma, I didn't stop to push the birds out of the road, I held onto her hand and ran to keep up with her strides. At the church Grandma got out her polish and rags and told us she would come back after her shopping. We could see the flower woman talking to the Reverend. The sun was shining through the stained glass windows and casting their shadows on the wall. They didn't notice us and we stayed at the back of the church and watched.

'She asked me to consecrate the courtyard of the fort for a bird cemetery. Imagine!' the Reverend said, resting a giant finger on his chin.

'Hmm' said the flower woman, and she pursed her giant lips. 'She should have left with everyone else when the Germans came, but she was always wilful.'

'I didn't know,' said the Reverend.

'She was a traitor and she got what she deserved,' said the flower woman. 'I saw her lying on the road in a pool of her own blood and I told the women that she'd had enough. It was a shame about the baby,' she said.

'I didn't know,' said the Reverend.

The shadows stopped moving and vanished as clouds blew over the sun. We heard the door of the church creaking open and we turned to see who it was. An old man came in with bundles of wilting flowers in soggy paper wrappings. He took a black sack off his shoulder and pushed them into it one by one. Sometimes he stopped and pulled a card out, and read it. He mouthed the words, but we couldn't make out what they were. Then he stuck the card in his pocket and carried on.

We heard something behind us and turned. The Reverend and the flower woman were walking towards us and we crouched down behind a pew.

'. . . in the courtyard,' said the Reverend.

'It could be anywhere,' said the flower woman.

When Grandma came we started for home. 'You can have a bag each,' she said, and we carried her shopping.

'Is the mad old woman all alone?' Esther asked.

'Yes,' Grandma said, and she took the bags out of our hands and told us to hurry, and we walked home in silence.

'Eat your greens,' Grandma said at supper and I cut them up and ate them with a piece of meat and potato, but it didn't hide the taste like rust.

'Where's Grandad buried?' Esther asked.

'They never found his body' Grandma said, and she shut her eyes. 'Eat your greens,' she said, and I ate another forkful.

That night we sat up in bed and watched while the light died away through the window. 'Who knocked her down on the road?' Esther said, looking into the black windows that framed the bay, and she got into my bed and we pulled the covers right over our heads. 'D'you think the bird's dead?' I said, and we rolled away from each other and tried to sleep.

Grandma said we should do a picture to send to our mother and I watched while Esther drew the bay. She put in the line of the wall, and the bands of sand and sea and sky, and hundreds of little black ticks, like birds.

'Why haven't you drawn the fort?' Grandma asked.

'I can't make it out from here.'

'You could imagine it,' Grandma said, and she went to water her geraniums.

'The Reverend said it was in the courtyard,' Esther said. I looked out across the bay, but the fort was hidden behind fog and the fog horn had started to moan. 'It could be anywhere,' I said.

But anywhere was a vast place to fit at the back of the mind, and we started walking towards the causeway. The wind had dropped and the sea was calm and it seemed as though we were the only things moving. We could barely see the fort until we came right up to it. The gates were just as they had been before, as though no-one had arrived or departed. We stepped into the courtyard. There were birds dotted everywhere, pecking at the seed scattered on the ground, and the noise was deafening. In the corner we could see an old piece of stone propped up against the wall, and in front of it a scattering of wild flowers. We walked towards it. 'Is that it?' I said. Esther didn't answer. She was looking up at the roof, and there was the mad old woman standing right on the edge and facing out to sea. She turned away from the wind and we saw something in her arms, and her head was bent towards it and she was whispering. The seagull opened its wings, spreading the bones like fingers, and she held it against her stomach with her large strong hands, and she fed it milk from a glass pipette, and she threw it into the air, and it flew.

GREGORY NORRIS

One Small Step

There is a golden rule in space travel: never take a child aged four. Seven – perfect, they'll love Mickey's moon hops at LunarDisney. Babies – fine, they'll just float in weightlessness, gurgling. But a four-year-old – that's asking for trouble.

And trouble is what I got from taking Katie for a fortnight at the Sea of Tranquillity. Her mother was off doing underwater archaeology at the submerged city of Amsterdam, while I was heading for my new job as manager of the lunar resort at Eagle Base. I could afford her million-dollar fare and thought the trip would be educational. A chance to see a bit of the solar system, an opportunity for father-daughter bonding. A stay on the moon would improve her vocabulary while low gravity would enhance her motor skills.

I had been warned. Her Development Programmes already graded her top decile in vocabulary and her co-ordination test scores were upper quadrant. Her only problem was the sub-optimal score for Civic Responsibility. As her grandmother put it: she kept getting into mischief.

It started the minute we reached earth orbit. Katie giggled when her long hair floated upwards and she was eager to play in weightlessness. She undid her straps.

'Look Daddy, I'm floating,' she cried.

'Don't spin,' I warned.

She promptly set herself tumbling head over heels. 'Oh, that makes me feel funny,' she said. I caught her just in time for her to throw up over me.

But the flight attendant vacuumed up with accustomed skill and Katie couldn't remain subdued for long. She tried to hide her smile but it crept back when she saw the earth rolling beneath us. I pointed out Japan, home of two of her grandparents, and she demanded the pilot take us over Madagascar so she could show everyone her house. On the day-long journey to the moon she became a favourite with the crew and passengers. She sat in the cockpit and flew for a while, sending the shuttle weaving through space, and for several hours refused to admit it was time for bed.

We woke just as we were reaching the moon for an initial sight-seeing orbit. The moonscape was stark, an almost abstract composition of craters and jagged peaks, and the intensity of the sunlight on the pristine surface contrasted with the velvet blackness of the shadows. Four billion years of stillness and silence made us all speak in whispers. Buzz Aldrin had summed it up perfectly as he stepped from the Eagle: 'Magnificent desolation.'

Katie was disappointed. 'Why doesn't it shine?' she asked. I explained in vain that the moon was one of the darkest objects in the solar system, reflecting only a fifth of the sun's light. When we landed she'd find moondust was dark grey.

'The moon does shine, I know it does, I've seen it from my bedroom window,' she proclaimed.

Suddenly the Sea of Tranquillity was below us and the shuttle's engines roared. The sunlight reflected off the polyethylene domes of Eagle Base, making them sparkle like diamonds amid the grey plains of the Maria. We could see the small size of this fragile outpost, surrounded by unrelenting hostility.

Katie forgot her disappointment as soon as we landed. A bus took us to the Columbia Hotel where she had her first try at walking in one-sixth g. The heavy carpet was not just for decoration, it acted as a shock absorber for new arrivals. She soon got the hang of running with long strides and moon-hops. 'Look, I'm a kangaroo,' she shouted.

Straight away we did what every tourist does first. We ignored LunarDisney and the bus tours and the views from the Skyway Lounge. The incredible low-g rollercoasters would have to wait, we'd try the swimming pool another day. Instead we headed for the Museum Dome.

It seems to draw you in. A sense of history catches you, the magical lure of those pioneering days. Ten years ago the pressurized dome was erected around the site to save visitors from peering through bus windows or clambering about in bulky space suite.

Now you feel closer, standing on a balcony in casual clothes, looking down over the scene.

And first of all you seek out the Footprint. After all it is the symbol of the Lunar Nation.

I pointed it out to Katie. 'There. At the foot of the ladder. Do you see?'

'Yes.' She wasn't impressed. 'It that it?'

'That's it.'

A footprint in the lunar dust, made by a clumsy boot with a rough tread. One of many that weave across the surface. It hardly seems possible this draws in tourists by the thousand. The greatest wonder of the solar system seems to be nothing but a small indentation.

But it's more. It's that first moment, it's that famous saying. Here was where it all began. You can't help but stare, marvel, salute.

Only after a few minutes can you take in the rest of the scene. The descent stage of the Eagle, the tiny capsule that brought Armstrong and Aldrin here so long ago, rests abandoned, its roof scorched when the ascent stage ignited and carried them home. The Stars and Stripes lies toppled in the dust, surrounded by more footprints where they struggled to plant it. A small plaque on a landing strut declares 'We came in peace for all mankind'. But your eyes always wander back to the Footprint.

Katie was getting bored. Looking around she asked, 'Why does it make everyone sad?'

I looked. Forty or so people were gathered around the balcony, all with glistening eyes. This was why they'd travelled a quarter of a million miles – they leant over the rail to be a little closer, they spoke in respectful whispers. We were all united in reverence: before us was the physical embodiment of the Giant Leap.

I directed Katie's attention to it once again. 'Do you like the Footprint?'

She gave it a few seconds' careful consideration. 'It's very big.' She flopped to the floor and pulled her feet to her face, giving grave inspection to the soles of her shoes. 'My feet are lots smaller.'

After a while we moon-hopped our way to the video hall and

laughed at the silly rockets and the comical Apollo spacesuits. It was all so primitive – not to mention dangerous.

'They came all this way just to make footprints?' asked Katie. And she was right: that was pretty much it. Armstrong and Aldrin only had a couple of hours on the moon, and much of that was wasted by a phone call from some President or other who wanted a chat. They grabbed a few lumps of rock, hammered in a seismometer and rushed home again. But somehow none of that seemed to matter. A footprint was enough.

The next day I had to get to grips with my new job and I delivered Katie to the care of the 'Moonbeams Club'. With a dozen other children she'd learn the club song and be taught a special Moonbeam walk – a kind of hopscotching hop and jump. There is nothing quite like the sense of peace that comes with handing over a four-year old to child-care professionals.

Not realising how short my tenure would be I started my new job with enthusiasm. A meeting with my assistants confirmed the main problem: the rival lunar resort, Falcon Base, was becoming a serious competitor. Their hotels overlooked the Apennine mountains and Hadley Rille canyon, giving stunning views. They too had a pioneer site: Apollo 15. Tourists crammed onto coaches to see the remains of the Falcon and the rover that Scott and Irwin rode across the lunar surface.

We had to admit their historical sights were awe-inspiring. A hammer and a falcon feather lay in the dust, dropped by Dave Scott in demonstration of Galileo's principal that objects fall together, no matter their weight. A small red Bible left on the rover's control panel symbolised the crew's faith. And a small plaque bearing the names of fourteen men had been left as a memorial to the cosmonauts and astronauts who'd died in that first decade of space exploration.

Falcon also offered more exciting activities – mountaineering up Bennet Peak, abseiling down into the Rille, racing on replicas of those absurd twentieth-century rovers. The latest James Bond movie had been filmed there and visitors wanted to copy the famous stunt of tobogganing down Silver Spur. I was still worrying about our rival when Katie returned home that evening.

'Look Daddy, they gave me a Moonbeams t-shirt and a badge!' she told me. 'Tomorrow we're going swimming at the Pleasure-Pool.'

Over the next few days Katie chatted away about her expeditions. She went on a tour of the local craters in a pressurised bus and tried a spacesuit to replicate the pioneers for a few minutes. She visited the greenhouses and became quite knowledgable about hydroponics. LunarDisney was her favourite. 'You should have seen it, Daddy, Mickey and Minnie did ballet dancing and Minnie got cross because Mickey kept bouncing away.'

Her daily report card hinted at additional adventures. 'Katie has been advised not to play in airlocks.' 'Katie has been told the nuclear reactor's access hatch is kept locked for a reason.' One evening she returned covered in moondust, the acrid gunpowder smell filling the hotel suite. Her report read: 'Katie should not use the experimental seed bed, vital to future lunar agriculture, as a sandpit.'

One day I was immersed in the resort's budget when the Class One Emergency siren reminded me of the awesome vulnerability of this human outpost. Of course it was a false alarm – there hadn't been an accident at Eagle Base for forty years – but it brought home the closeness of the pure vacuum, the horrors of depressurisation, the danger of fire. As I rushed to the emergency oxygen packs I was reminded of the terrible price paid to create this paradise, starting with the three astronauts of Apollo One burning inside their tiny capsule. The false alarm left me even more in admiration of those pioneering days.

That evening Katie's report read: 'Katie should not press the Class One Emergency alarm, even if her Barbie doll has been exposed to the vacuum without its space suit.' I wasn't sure Katie listened but I tried to explain the dangers that others had endured for her present enjoyment, attempting to emphasise the legacy of the pioneers that gave her this vacation on the moon.

'All they did was make a Footprint,' she said. 'I don't see what's dangerous about that. Barbie was out in the vacuum in nothing but her bikini.'

'Those Footprints are humankind's greatest achievement,' I said. But I knew my words were wasted.

It was on the following day that Katie became famous across the solar system. I worked late into the evening, assuming she'd be OK at the crèche. I was finishing a report concluding the rival Falcon resort would never catch Eagle Base – market research showed we'd always be the preferred tourist destination because we had the Footprint. That indentation in the dust guaranteed our billion-dollar-a-day profit.

Then I got the call. Katie was missing.

I ended up the villain but the Moonbeams Club teachers were the ones to blame. How can trained professional let a four-year old go wandering off at the end of the day?

My heart raced. I had visions of her outside on the lunar surface or trapped in an airlock. I grew a little calmer when the security personnel confirmed all the tour buses had returned and all space suits and moon buggies were accounted for. The most dangerous parts of the resort were checked and found clear.

It was a while before I thought of the Museum Dome. Maybe my lecture the previous evening had been successful after all. Perhaps Katie, filled at last with a sense of her heritage, had wanted another look.

I hurried there, bounding with the longest hops as I could manage. The museum had been shut for some time and my calls echoed through the exhibits. To my disappointment I found the viewing area deserted.

Then I heard a sound from below. How she'd got down there I've never discovered.

I lent over the balcony. The tracks of the Apollo astronauts were overlaid by the marks of much smaller shoes. A trail of tiny footprints weaved around the Eagle and they showed the unmistakable pattern of the Moonbeams hopscotch walk.

I looked towards the Footprint. You can imagine my relief when I saw it was still intact.

But above it a small figure jumped from the Eagle's ladder. She floated down towards the Footprint, feet braced for impact.

'Look Daddy,' she cried. I can make footprints too.'

LINDA THOMPSON

Midnight in Seville

I was twelve years old when my sister died. She was fifteen. Her heart stopped one morning as she stepped onto a bus and she fell back into the arms of an absolute stranger. Why Lisa, our parents cried, why did it have to be Lisa? The real question, of course, was why couldn't it have been me? If it had to be anyone, why not take the dull one? But God always was picky. Some of us aren't cut out to be sunbeams in heaven.

This is not to say Mum and Dad didn't love me. I was deluged by love and their need to protect me. But I was a realist even then and understood how natural it was for the thought to cross their minds. Mum locked Lisa's bedroom. Its emptiness created a dark, silent gulf between my room and theirs.

My parents' oppressiveness can still haunt me, almost thirty years on. They bundled me to the doctor, who pronounced me fit. Yet Dad insisted on driving me to and from school. For almost a year he did without a lunch break so that he could leave the office early and bring me safely home. This interfered with his work and made him anxious. I noticed his popping white knuckles as he gripped the wheel. He whistled incessantly in that tight-lipped way, sifting air through his teeth. The car stank of cigarettes, cheesy sock, stifled leather. I'd sit primly beside him, my temples tingling from where Mum had smoothed back my fringe, the wet ring of her kiss still alight on my forehead. She said goodbye to me each morning as if it might be my last. This made me a bit nervous; aware of God's predilection for cherished children, I felt marked for slaughter.

'It's horrible in this car,' I told Dad once. 'It stinks and I could suffocate and then you'd be sorry!'

He wound down the window.

'Right! There's your air, you nasty little sod. No child of mine dies with me around. Do you hear me? Eh?'

I nodded dumbly. I wanted to tell him his anger was a breath of fresh air.

Outside the car, normal life carried on without us. Unmindful of our loss, the postman emptied the postbox; bread was being delivered to Sayers on the square. We passed my friends, strolling, running, trotting backwards, sharing jokes and secrets, not missing me at all. I'd press my face against the window, wondering if this was how it felt to be dead, segregated from the living, invisible, alone.

I'd never really worked through my grief over Lisa. Of course, I'd cried because she'd gone. But the subtleties of grieving weren't expected of me, somehow. You're lucky, people said, you're a child, you can cry. Look at your poor parents. They must wipe their eyes and carry on regardless. They're marvellous, you know. They've lost a lovely, clever daughter. Can anything be worse? With hindsight, I might have told them losing a sister came close – a bossy nuisance of a sister who'd always stolen my thunder. I missed her like a headache, like leaves miss rain. But I closed the door on my feelings, just as Mum closed the door on Lisa's bedroom. I imagined she was still in there, bent industriously over her homework or lying sulkily on her bed after a row with Dad. I'd even tiptoe past, not wanting to disturb her. It became a sort of game.

Deep down, I knew I needed to go in, though at the time it seemed a bit of a dare. Mum had hidden the key inside the evening gloves she never wore any more. I remember sliding open the drawer in her dresser. The long, black gloves were folded within themselves, their fingers waving like a tail. I delved into the velvet centre and traced the key's warm, curved edge. It felt incredibly naughty. I caught my reflection in the mirror. My usually peaky face was transfigured by delight. Even my mouse-brown hair glowed with possibilities. I wonder if I sat forever in the sun, I might become a red-blonde like Lisa.

The key didn't jam as I'd feared and turned easily in the lock. A giggle juddered from my throat as I gripped the handle. It was a Sunday afternoon, hot and hazy. Sounds carried on the air. Mum and Dad were in the garden. The landing window was open and I could hear the chop of Mum's hoe. I could just about see Dad digging over the top border, the back of his neck, even at that distance, looking lividly sore. I pressed the handle down a little further, so that the latch gave but did not quite click free. My heart hammered against my ribs. The door opened with a deafening crack, like a shot from a gun. I was sure they must have heard it. I didn't want to turn round, didn't want to see Dad throw down his spade and come pelting down the garden. Mum's hoeing stopped, along with my heart, but only for a second, or maybe two. I took a deep, grateful breath. The only way was forward. It had to be now.

The room was an oven. A faint whiff of orange teetered as I entered. It was Lisa's perfume, 'Midnight in Seville'. My eyes darted to the economy-sized spray still towering on the dressing-table. 'Midnight in Seville' – all the girls wore it. Dad had really hated it.

'God help them in Seville,' he'd jibed, 'If that's what it smells like.'

I guessed he must be sorry now, sorry he had said that. And then panic seized me. I had left the door open. I was letting her go, letting her essence drift onto the landing, through the open window, out onto the air. It was as if she were dying all over again. I ran to the door and slammed it shut, not caring if they'd heard me. I'd saved her, that was the main thing, kept her here where she belonged.

Lisa's bedroom was bigger than mine and looked out onto our avenue, at a row of semis more or less identical to ours. Nothing much had changed; the walls were still plastered with posters of Kevin Keegan, black-haired, red-shirted, iconised. Here was the yellow and black Gonk Auntie Maureen had knitted; Lisa's brushes and combs; lipsticks; radio; her dressing-gown on the door. Yet I was struck by a sense of unfamiliarity. In retrospect, I could say I was like a tourist visiting a shrine in a foreign country. Of course the analogy would have been lost on me then, because I'd never been abroad. But I felt grimy, unworthy, as if I didn't belong. Only Mum had been in since Lisa died. She'd tidied up her clothes, plumped up her spooky-white pillows. Swept the dust away. The pristine room seemed to wait for Lisa's return. Her bursting school bag was on the desk, expecting her to open it. What on earth was it thinking? Didn't it remember being dropped in the gutter when she died?

I turned to Kevin, all the pictures of Kevin – Kevin on one knee, grinning for the camera, Kevin chasing the ball, Kevin leaping and triumphantly punching the air. I covered my eyes. *Kevin,* I whispered, *there's something I must tell you. It's something very sad, so you've got to be brave. But life is very sad sometimes, you know that don't you? Lisa is dead. It is true, Kevin . . . I'm sorry . . . it is. Nobody told you. Lisa is dead.* I opened my eyes into the dark of my palms and saw the anguish on his face as he sank to the ground. This was not the Kevin worshipped by thousands, but Lisa's own Kevin, the Kevin who shared her secrets, inhabited this room, who would wait no more for his love to come home.

Dad was banging about in the kitchen. I could picture him clearly, searching cupboards for a glass, as if he were a stranger. I prepared to make myself scarce. Then the oddest thing happened; my body acted directly against my inclination to escape. I strolled to the dressing-table, picked up the perfume, uncapped it and sprayed it on my neck. Its cold squirt made me squeal. I closed my eyes and mouth tight and felt its tiny, scented needles pricking through my skin. I barely knew what I had done. It felt deliciously dangerous. I would leave the room reeking of Lisa's perfume.

As I returned the spray to the dressing-table, I paused for a moment. It occurred to me I had lost track of Dad's movements downstairs. Had he left the kitchen, returned to the garden? Or had he followed his nose, been drawn by some intuition out into the hallway? Perhaps he was listening there now, head cocked to one side. If I moved one muscle, I would give myself away. For what seemed like an eternity, I stood frozen to the spot. It felt like we were stalking, each waiting for the other to make the first move. I imagined him stretching his hand out, by degrees, to clutch the banister, making ready to propel himself onto the stairway at the very first second he heard the floorboards creak. I grew tired in the end, my thighs felt dithery. I realized that if I didn't do something, my absence would be noticed anyway. With my back to the wall, I edged to the door and opened it carefully. Through the window, I could see Dad back at his post at the top of the garden, leaning on his spade, gazing away from the house into the distance somewhere. I crept from the room and locked the door behind me.

From then on, I visited the room whenever I could. The visits had to be short, because my parents never left me in the house alone. As I entered I always made straight for 'Midnight in Seville'. To spray it on my skin was an exquisite liberation, gave me leave to touch her things. Only then could I perform the small task I had set myself in my limited time. Perhaps I'd try on her shoes; once I used her hairbrush so that some of my own brown hairs mingled with her golden ones, still entangled in the bristles. The perfume permeated my being, to the extent that I could feel my appearance had changed. The transformation wasn't permanent, but it was profound in its way. There were moments when I knew I looked like Lisa and that if, at that split second, someone had entered the room, they'd have seen Lisa, not me. I tried at first to catch her in the mirror, but she was gone in a blink. This seemed natural and right; I wasn't fazed by it at all. As I left the room I was taking her with me. I'd rehearse her walk across the landing, her confident stride; I felt the swish of her ponytail as I tossed my head. My pulse would race as I entered the living-room. When our parents looked up, which one of us would they see? If they were seeing Lisa, this was courtesy of me; I was the real one, setting her spirit free.

One day, at tea-time, Dad sniffed the air suddenly, a bit greedily, like a dog. He looked at Mum accusingly.

'God – you're not wearing her scent now!'

'No, Dave – but I can smell it!'

They glanced at me briefly, then across at Lisa's empty place, a mixture of wonderment and fear in their faces. It couldn't possibly have been me wearing the perfume; they wanted it to be Lisa, desperately needing to fill that space on her chair. I made a performance of sniffing about me.

'Yes – I can smell it too!' I cried, slightly overdoing it. 'It's that orangey stuff Lisa used to wear – I can't remember what it's called.'

'Midnight in Seville,' Dad said quietly. He scraped back his chair and left the table.

Mum seemed to take the haunting calmly; I guessed she had Lisa where she wanted her, close at hand. I worried more about Dad. He began to look pale and strained, glancing about him as he entered a room. I longed to come clean. But I knew that this would mean the end of my visits. And I could no more stop my visits that die myself.

Dad must have felt tormented, as if Lisa were punishing him with the perfume he hated so much. He and Lisa had clashed a lot. As she'd grown up, he'd become over-protective and critical of her friends. They'd had a row on the morning she died and I don't think he ever absolved himself of this. Sometimes, when we stopped at the Kwik Save lights, the girls from Our Lady's would cross the road in front of us. There was one with stunning hair, similar to Lisa's. I felt the churn of my heart as Dad turned away and gazed across at the 'Special Offer' flyers. The girl might be laughing, unaware of her impact. Dad's shrill whistling would transform into a hum that seemed dark in comparison and stung me with pity.

At the end of term, we finished school at lunch time. They'd given us letters several weeks before, advising our parents of the arrangements. I'd mislaid mine somewhere, forgotten it completely, whether by accident or design I was never quite certain. Mum did mornings at the local chemist and, by a stroke of luck, was visiting Auntie Maureen straight from work. I forewent the opportunity to join my friends on the bus, because I didn't want to be diverted from my plan for the afternoon. Instead, I persuaded Sharon Jackson's mother to give me a lift. Aware of our family history, she wasn't that keen and asked if I was sure my parents would agree to it. I nodded vigorously and assured Mrs Jackson that they trusted her to bring me home in one piece. My deception was convincing. I even called out to Mum as I opened the door and waved cheerfully from the step, praying all the time that Mrs Jackson would not get out to try to justify her action. She drove away at last, tentatively waving. I had the house to myself for the very first time.

I stood in Lisa's room not knowing what to do. I wasn't used to such freedom. Time stretched out into limitless space. I looked at Kevin, then beyond him at the jubilant crowd and had a flash of inspiration. What this room needed, I decided, was to be filled with noise. I couldn't think of a song, so I sang LA-LA-LA! at the top of my voice. Then, in true poltergeist style, I began to open and shut drawers, pull the curtains back and forth. I kicked off my shoes and scrambled onto the bed, wildly trampolining, leaping like Kevin, punching the air like Kevin, punching it, punching it. I lost my balance in the end and staggered to a standstill, clutching the window sill for support. My heart was racing like an overwound watch, which might stop any second. I had to take it easy. I didn't want to die.

Lisa's neatly folded nightie had partly slid from the pillow. I sank to my knees and crawled slowly towards it, as if it were some creature uncoiling for attack. If only I could flip that one end back into place, no one would notice. It slithered from the mound just as I stretched out my hand. I leapt from the bed, as if I'd been bitten. The nightie lay crumpled in front of me. I spread it out and stepped back from it for a moment. It was in that oyster shade that brides often wear; Lisa wasn't one for trendy nightshirts. I stroked it gently; it was lovely to touch. The fabric was soft and fluid not given easily to folding. I would never be able to emulate Mum's deft control. Unfolding Lisa's nightie was a point of no return. Now it was unfolded, there was no taking it back. I had nothing to lose now, nothing at all.

Without a second thought, I peeled off my uniform and my underwear too. It was like shedding a skin, several skins in fact, layer upon layer of rough, scratchy skin. My body felt moist and utterly new. I wasn't a child any more. I could do what I wanted. I picked up the nightie. I put it over my head and held up my arms, so that it poured silkily down my back like pure spring water. I pulled back the covers and slid into Lisa's bed. The pillow puffed round my ears like virgin snow.

I lay on my side and took deep, sleepy breaths. But something wasn't quite right. As I breathed out, the atmosphere seemed overbearingly weighted with orange. I closed my mouth firmly. It wasn't coming from me. A second breath shadowed each of mine, was fluttering now on my neck and shoulders. Someone was with me, next to me in bed. I knew it was Lisa, definitely Lisa. When we were little, we slept together on holiday. She had this habit of burrowing into my back, seeking the warmth and comfort that bodily contact brings. It was the only time I'd ever experienced her dependency. And I felt it now, more intensely than ever. Instinct told me not to try to turn round, that she was not how I remembered her. There was an icy delicacy about the form that clung to me, an absence of bone. I sensed it craved my humanity, the heat from my blood, yet still in its memory was a need for me too.

Scared as I was, I didn't want to let go of her. Whatever was happening, I had to give in to it. I closed my eyes and inhaled 'Midnight in Seville'. Each breath took us further into scented darkness; we circumnavigated sphere upon sphere of impossible space. We found a beach at the core of it, some stars, a moon. I conjured up a tree, so laden with fruit its boughs were dipping, closer and closer to my outstretched hand. Even though it was midnight, the oranges burned brightly, bewitchingly lit like Halowe'en lanterns. *Stretch higher*, Lisa whispered. *Remember your body is all that we have.* I grasped at an orange. It was heavy with life and took two hands to hold. It beat like a heart. I pressed the fruit to my lips and bit through the skin. I felt the soft yield beneath, the light burst in my mouth. *That's right*, Lisa said. *Hold on to the sensation . . . hold on to it . . . hold . . . .*

Something pierced my consciousness. I was confused for a moment. I heard the shattering of glass and Dad cursing. So that's what it was. Dad slammed the front door and the loose pane had fallen out. I took the knowledge calmly, then I heard him call my name. The predicament I was in suddenly dawned on me. Dad was taking the stairs two at a time, his voice stark with anxiety. As I struggled to get up, my foot caught in the sheet and I tumbled out of bed. The thud stopped Dad abruptly in his flight. I could almost hear what he was thinking. He called my name again, but this time as a question. *Is it you?* his tone said. *Is it you or . . .?* I had little choice but to scramble to my feet and wait for him to enter. There was no time for deception. Between nudity and Lisa's nightie, the nightie seemed preferable.

At the sight of me, Dad took a step back as if avoiding a blow. His eyes scanned my body at least three or four times before believing their own evidence. It took a while for him to speak.

'Peter! What in hell's name are you playing at?'

It was difficult to think of an acceptable answer. I felt suddenly chilled and began to tremble involuntarily. Dad dashed towards me and grabbed hold of my arm, more violently I think than he really intended. The jolt made me cry out, so he loosened his grip and placed his other hand under my elbow.

'Look at me, Peter.'

I looked first at his hands, the spiky hair on the backs of them, his cracked, neglected nails. They felt hefty and rough. He might just as well have been wearing chainmail gloves. I raised my eyes obediently to his face, though I didn't really want to, because I knew it would be thin and painfully old. All the red in his hair had been painted out. His green eyes like a cat's had faded, despite the panic and anger which now glowed there, the thread of tenderness too.

'Listen to me! Go and take the damn thing off and never – ever – do this again. Do you hear me?'

'Yes, Dad. Sorry.'

He let go of my arm and pressed his hand against my back to guide me to the door.

'And as for this . . . bloody . . . fiasco!' I turned in response. Kevin was grinning agreeably as Dad waved his arms at the contents of the room. 'This has all got to go – and I mean NOW!!' He grabbed the bedclothes and flung them to the floor.

I dashed to my own bedroom. I didn't want to watch, yet I felt exhilarated too because something was changing. So Dad had wanted change too; I couldn't believe it. He was swearing his head off, dragging drawers open, rattling hangers as he divested them of clothes. When Mum came home there would be hell to pay, but the storm had broken, was clearing the air. I took the nightie off and pressed it gratefully to my face. Then I rolled it up and stowed it at the back of my wardrobe.

My parents almost parted in the following weeks, before Mum could allow the dust to settle on Lisa's room. Then she set to work cleaning, re-inventing the space for me. The move brought me physically nearer to my parents, closed the gap between us. The bigger bedroom gave me status too. I was the only one, as opposed to the one who was left. If made a difference, believe me.

I never told them about my encounter with Lisa and assume Dad chose to forget the episode with the nightie. I continued to wear it whenever things got tough. It helped my put things in perspective. In that nightie I'd weathered the worst crisis of my life, traversed impassable borders. What could possibly worry me?

As time went on, the scent of oranges faded. It became less Lisa's nightie, more a relic of the past. I shoved it in a bag Mum had left out for the Salvation Army.

The Captain called to collect the bag as I was tying it up again. She complimented me on my efforts in a worthy cause. I smiled at her pleasantly and folded my arms across my chest. The cold, secreted silk spread beneath my jumper. How could I have thought of letting it go?

Biographies

The Judges

Lynne Reid Banks wrote several plays and was one of the first female news reporters at ITN before turning her hand to novel writing – creating her memorable first novel, *The L-Shaped Room.* Since then she has produced a great body of work for both adults and children and her classic children's story, *The Indian in the Cupboard*, was recently made into a movie.

George Szirtes has published twelve volumes of poetry, including most recently *Portrait of my Father in an English Landscape* (OUP, 1998), which is both a PBS recommendation and a Book of the Year. He has won or been short-listed for many major awards including the Faber Memorial Prize, the Whitbread Poetry Prize, the Wiedenfeld Prize and the Forward Prize for Poetry.

The Winners

Simon Back has been writing fiction since junior school but seriously only in the past four years. He grew up in Leicestershire and moved to Nottingham after graduating from Loughborough University in 1996. He has completed one novel and is working on another.

Lesley Byers, originally from Lancashire, worked in the fashion and international automotive businesses before retiring to have children. She now lives in Bournemouth with her husband and two daughters. She has published *In Your Own Time*, a collection of dramatic duologues and monologues for young people. A novel and more short stories are in the pipeline.

Mike Casey has worked and taught in Dublin, Washington and Cambridge. He has won awards for poetry and short fiction and has published a novel in which the main character never appears.

Dennis Casling lives and works in the West Country and has won prizes and been published in several anthologies.

Brian Clover grew up in London, but spent 1973–76 teaching English in Dorchester and Weymouth. Since then, he has worked as a researcher, analyst, manager and lecturer, but has also contributed topical jokes and sketches to BBC Radio. This is his first poetry competition. He has just finished writing a play about comics and is currently working on one about poets.

Valerie Darville began writing poetry seriously only ten years ago after the break-up of her marriage. She lives in north London with her partner, Anthony and cat, Oz. She occasionally reads at the Salisbury House Poets' evenings in Enfield and at Torriano's in London.

Jane Draycott lives in Oxfordshire. Her first full collection, *Prince Rupert's Drop* (Carcanet/OUP, 1999) was shortlisted for the 1999 Forward Prize. In 1998 she co-wrote *Christina the Astonishing* (Two Rivers Press) with poet Lesley Saunders and artist Peter Hay. A previous pamphlet, *No Theatre* (Smith/Doorstop), was shortlisted for the 1997 Forward Prize for Best First Collection.

Dodie Ellis comes from Kendal in the Lake District but has lived in a Northamptonshire village for nearly 13 years. She has a husband and son who put up with her passion for writing. She has had many stories published in magazines and has won three *Writers Forum* story prizes. She won second prize in the Petra Kenney Poetry Competition in 1996, and has written three plays, two of which have been performed by excellent amateur groups.

Nigel Forde began his career as an actor at York Theatre Royal and has stayed in the area ever since. He co-founded Riding Lights Theatre Co. He has contributed to many BBC radio programmes and is best known for presenting Radio 4's *Bookshelf.* He now works primarily as a writer, and a musical, written with Arnold Wesker, was premiered in Japan in 2000.

He wrote the screenplay for three of BBC2's animated series *Testament*, one of which was nominated for a BAFTA and won an EMMY, and two films in Norman Stone's series, 'Tales from the Madhouse'. His seven books to date include three of poetry and a critical anthology of G.K.Chesterton. His children's play, *Beauty and the Beast*, is to be produced at the Polka Theatre at Christmas 2000 and the New Year.

Ann-Marie Fyfe was born in Cushendall on the Antrim coast and now lives with her husband and two children in London. She teaches English and Creative Writing at Richmond-upon-Thames College, runs the poetry reading series at The Troubadour in Earls Court and has published research on contemporary Irish women's writing.

Her poems first appeared in *London Magazine* in 1993, and her poems, essays and reviews have since appeared in a wide range of literary magazines. In 1998 she was a prize-winner in the *Daily Telegraph* Arvon International Poetry Competition, and *A House by the Sea*, a short sequence of poems set against the Atlantic coastline, was published in 1995. Her recently published work includes a collection, *Late Crossing* (Rockingham, 1999) and a second collection is due from the same publishing house in July 2001.

Rebecca Goss, 26, was originally from Suffolk but now lives in Liverpool. Her pamphlet collection, *Keeping Houston Time*, was published by Slow Dancer Press in 1997. Her poems have appeared, and are forthcoming, in various national anthologies and magazines including *Ambit* and *London Magazine*. She teaches creative writing part-time at Liverpool John Moores University.

Tracy Horn is 38 years old, and although raised in Johannesburg, South Africa and in Margate she considers herself a Londoner. Her occupations are philosopher, teacher and writer; her main influences Blake and Spinoza.

Sian Hughes was born in 1965 Previous publications include *Saltpetre*, Smith/Doorstop Books, 1997, and *Poems on the Underground*, 1996. More recent work has appeared in *London Magazine, Poetry Review* and the *TLS*. In 2000 she received a Southern Arts Writer's Award.

Ann Jolly spent her childhood in Glasgow and now lives near Chichester, working as a probation officer and yoga teacher. She has written for her own pleasure since she could hold a pencil and after spending 1995 living, working and writing in rural Tanzania she has had several short stories published in anthologies and was 1999 winner of the Asham Award.

Kathryn Kupla is a fiction writer, librarian and editor. She lives in Middletown, Rhode Island, USA on the Atlantic coast. Her stories have appeared in *Madison Review, Larcom Review, Minimus, Parting Gifts*, *Pif* and *Leviathan* in the USA, in *Les Episodes* in France, and in *Quality Women's Fiction* in the UK. Another story, 'How the Light Walks', won the 2000 *Florida Review* Editor's Award in fiction.

Paul Lee began writing poetry some five years ago, at the age of 43, for reasons he still does not understand. He is married to Emma Lee, also a poet, and a short story writer and reviewer. Both are widely published in the small poetry press.

James MacIlravie finished his degree and a year's postgraduate course in 1998 and then worked for a year on a Helpdesk. He is currently working on an illustrated book. He says poetry isn't a hobby or an interest, more a way of thinking.

Gregory Norris has won a number of short story contests in the past year, including the Burmah Castrol/*Reader's Digest* competition and the Guildford Book Festival competition. His stories have been published in *World Wide Writers, Cadenza, Real Writers 1999* and other publications. He recently won the Nancy Smith Memorial Trophy for the start of his second novel and is currently rewriting his first.

Mario Petrucci won last year's Bridport competition with his poem 'Negatives', written during his time at the Imperial War

Museum as their first poet in residence. He is completing a Year-of-the-Artist project in Havering, writing site-specific poems for public display on billboards, and has just started a Royal Literary Fellowship at Oxford Brookes University.

Ben Portus is training to be a veterinary surgeon at the University of Bristol and has a BSc in Equine Science. He has an unpublished collection of short stories and is currently working on a novel based on his experiences as a volunteer at a Guatemalan orphanage. He has written several scientific articles, and was a finalist in the 20–28 years category of the *Daily Telegraph* Young Science Writer Awards 2000.

Chris Powell was born in Surrey and now lives in County Durham. She is in the second year of an MA in Creative Writing at the University of Northumbria, teaches drama and has recently been awarded an Arts Council 'Year of the Artist' grant to be writer-in-residence at the Stanhope and Weardale Co-operative Society.

Linda Rogers is a Canadian poet, who also writes fiction, non-fiction and children's books. With her husband, mandolinist Rick van Krugel, she writes and performs songs for children. Mother of three sons, she has two grandchildren. She reviews books on the evening news and teaches writing workshops and on contract with various universities and online. She is Past President of the League of Canadian Poets and has been awarded the Stephen Leacock Poetry Prize, the Dorothy Livesay Poetry Prize, the Prix Anglais (France), the Voices Israel Award and the Acom Rukeyser Award (USA) and was Victoria Arts Citizen of the Year in 1998. Her greatest concern is for the rights of children.

Gill Saxon is a former newspaper journalist. Born in Sparkbrook, Birmingham in 1956, she now lives in Cambridge and is a recent English graduate of Cambridge University's Lucy Cavendish College. Gill writes drama and short stories as well as poetry and her work has appeared in the *Oxford and Cambridge May Anthologies*, on local radio and on several Cambridge stages. Her most recent venture is a comedy feature-film script involving *Feng Shui* and designer babies.

Pauline Stainer has published five collections with Bloodaxe. *The Wound-dresser's Dream* was short-listed for the Whitbread Poetry Prize, and her most recently collection, *Parable Island*, evokes the land- and sea-scapes of Orkney, where she lived until recently. She now lives in Suffolk.

Domini Stallings was born in 1972 and lives in London. She has recently completed an MA in Creative Writing at the University of Sussex. This is her first publication.

David Swann used to reckon his name was a corruption of 'Sven' and that his ancestors were Vikings. He now accepts that 'Swann' derives from 'swine farmer' and that the name of his birthplace, Accrington, means 'Acorn Town'. He now lives in Brighton, with his soul-mate Angela, and teaches at University College, Chichester. This is his second success in the Bridport Prize.

Gordon Taylor is a poet living in Toronto. He works for a major financial institution but pursues his interest in poetry and music in his spare time. His poems have been published in several small literary journals in Canada.

Linda Thompson lives in the north-west of England. Her work has been broadcast and anthologised and she has twice been a prize-winner in the Northern Short Story Competition. Last year, she was awarded an MA in Writing from Liverpool John Moores University. She is currently revising a novel and preparing a collection of stories.

Marcy Willow studied English Literature and did her Master's Degree in Creative Writing at the University of Oregon. She has taught poetry and fiction writing. She lives with her two children in New England, where together they play baseball and climb mountains; they visit friends in Britain as often as they can. She won the 1994 Bridport Prize for Fiction, and was on the Arc Fiction Prize Short List in 1995. She is currently working on a novel.

Ceri Worman was born in 1958 in Cardiff but most of her formative years were spent in Barnsley. She studied history at Hull University and librarianship at Aberystwyth. She has worked as a children's librarian in Slough, Richmond and Wandsworth. After the birth of her son, Marcus in 1991, she became a teacher of English in London and is now teaching in Montevideo, Uruguay. She has only recently been able to concentrate on writing and this Bridport Prize is her first success.

Victoria Worsley was born in London in 1966. Since leaving Oxford in 1988, she has worked mainly as an actor and runs Jade, a new-writing theatre company she founded in 1992. On the writing side, she began by co-devising shows with cult performance company Tattycoram in the 1980s, since when she has written two plays toured by Jade and a short piece, *Lift and Separate*, commissioned and produced by Soho Theatre Company and published this year by Faber & Faber in *Mythic Women/Real Women.* Prose fiction is a recent departure; this is the second short story she has submitted to competition. Her first, *Crossing the Line*, reached the short list for the Assam Award in 1999 and has been optioned as a short film script by Ideal World in Glasgow.

Howard Wright is a lecturer in art history at the University of Ulster at Belfast. Currently, he has poems in *Writing Ulster*, *The Edinburgh Review*, *The Black Mountain Review* and *HU*. He also reviews poetry.